"Wherever the minist
ral is sure to follow.
to live in the middle o
through my friend William McDowell."

Steven Furtick, pastor, Elevation Church; New York Times
bestselling author

"The anointing and presence of God is real! William is not only a friend but a mentor, and I cannot wait for the words of God to flow through your heart, mind, body and spirit. The Holy Spirit is alive and well not only in this book but also in William's life, church and songs. I pray that before you read this powerful book you will say a prayer for Jesus to open up your heart and soul to this spiritual journey you are about to go on! This journey will be overflowing with joy, tears and the presence of Jesus from beginning to end."

Russell Wilson, quarterback, Seattle Seahawks

"God is using William McDowell and Deeper Fellowship Church to be a prophetic signpost in this generation. In the tension between seeking God's presence and seeking to be cool, they're favoring His presence. And He's honoring that with miracles. May you be infected with the spirit of faith that permeates this book."

Bob Sorge, author, Secrets of the Secret Place

"When he was a young man, sitting in the back of the auditorium in my meetings, William McDowell's gift may have been unknown to me, but it certainly was not unknown to God. It has been a tremendous privilege for me to observe his growth and development in so many different areas—as a husband, father, pastor, songwriter, worshiper and, now, as an author. It is gratifying, but not at all surprising, to see how God is using him, not only as an unusually gifted worship leader but also as a caring and compassionate pastor whose services are characterized by a remarkable demonstration of the supernatural power of God."

Dr. Rod Parsley, pastor and founder,
World Harvest Church, Columbus, Ohio

"I am so excited about the miracles taking place at Deeper Fellowship through Pastor William McDowell's ministry. He's shaking the culture and experiencing God's power on earth as it is in heaven and seeing wonderful miracles as a result. I love his heart for God. The posture of a church that stays in God's presence will always experience heaven! This book will turn hearts to God! I am glad to call this man of God my friend!"

Erica Campbell, host, *Get Up! Mornings with Erica Campbell*; recording artist, Mary Mary

"It's hard to believe that I've only known William McDowell for a handful of years when the impact of his ministry on my life has been exponential. Out of the many conversations we have had, one statement stood out to me more than any other. He told me that if we say what the Father says, He'll make a way for His Word. The impact of that one sentence has reverberated in my life, and I credit it with much of the success I've had. I'm grateful not only for William's friendship but also his ability to demonstrate a life tangibly connected to the heart of God. I know that this book and his ministry will have the same effect on all those who read with open hearts, and I'm excited about the new season so many people will walk into because of it."

Danny Gokey, GRAMMY-nominated Christian artist

"Pastor William McDowell has given his life to listening to the Holy Spirit as he has fashioned prophetic songs that address the family of God's desire to express their deepest feelings of worship. That same ability to hear and write songs of worship is now finding expression in revelatory teaching and preaching that has produced a faith to believe for the regular visitation of the Holy Spirit in their home church."

Joseph L. Garlington Sr., presiding bishop, Reconciliation! Ministries International

"From the moment I met William McDowell, humility and faithfulness oozed out of him. The same can be said when you begin to experience this book. It's truly an encouragement toward greater faith and a challenge not to miss what God has happening in your life!"

Josh McCown, NFL quarterback

"Too often Christians are willing to do a God thing without God. My friend William is the exact opposite. He refuses to continue going through the Christian motions without seeing and hearing from God. His relentless pursuit has been rewarded as God continues to pour out His presence and miracles. I thank God for who William is to the Kingdom of God at large and to the people who are privileged to call him friend."

Jonathan Stockstill, lead pastor, Bethany Church,
Baton Rouge, Louisiana

"When I discovered that William McDowell had begun pastoring a church, I was so excited I moved my entire family to a different city just to be close enough to attend the church when my ministry was not on the road. Not too many people outside of those we read about in the book of Acts have had that much of an impact on my life. Writing this, I feel like Peter in 2 Peter 1:16. I am an eyewitness of the revival that is taking place in the church that William leads."

Jonathan Ferguson, founder, Ferguson Global Ministries

"I have been blessed by the mantle of praise and worship William McDowell is known for, and I have been to Deeper Fellowship Church and experienced firsthand the power of God in the atmosphere under his leadership. What's happening there is a beautiful fulfillment of God's promises in Act 2:17 and Mark 16:17–19. I pray the accounts documented in this book will bring life to the reader and ignite faith like wildfire within the Church worldwide. To God be the glory!"

Jackie Patillo, president and executive director,
Gospel Music Association

"I have known William for over thirty years. When he was a young teenager it was evident that, through his musical gifts, he had a calling on his life to touch the world. It is no surprise that he has been raised up as one of the leading worship pastors in this generation. Now as a senior pastor, William has chosen to courageously lead his congregation outside the lines of tradition and conformity, and in so doing, they are experiencing what it truly looks like when heaven touches earth! I am honored to know William and to see how God is using him to bring His Kingdom to earth. May it happen *everywhere*!"

John W. Stevenson, apostle and senior pastor,
Heirs Covenant Church, Hamilton, Ohio

"My experience with the ministry of William McDowell has been powerful and enriching. His passion for God and worship have impacted me and the church I lead in unbelievable ways!"

John Jenkins Sr., pastor, First Baptist Church,
Glenarden, Maryland

"I've been able to see the disabled walk, the sick be healed, frowns turned to smiles. The presence at Deeper Fellowship is hard to put into words, but when you are present you understand just how impactful and loving of a home it is. What I love is how Pastor William doesn't move until he knows the Holy Spirit has moved in the way He's supposed to."

Tobias Harris, forward, Detroit Pistons

"God has positioned Pastor William McDowell with a mantle of miracles and a grace to release revival among the nations. The grace God has put on his life is a unique threefold cord of prophetic worship, fervent prayer and holy manifestation of God's presence. The message he carries calls a generation of sons and daughters closer to the heart of God. As a man after God's own heart, Pastor William is marked by the humility and kindness that he exudes while carrying this mantle of revival across the nations."

Kevin Wallace, lead pastor, Redemption to the Nations Church

"Pastor William McDowell is an amazing friend and a most esteemed Kingdom partner. His love for God's people shows in everything he does. Pastor McDowell has maintained a keen level of precision in leading God's people because his ear remains fastened to the mouth of God. He is a refreshing and much-needed vessel who understands the methodology required to release the power of God in the earthly realm. I am a firm believer that the earth will yield the increase of Pastor McDowell's anointing for years to come."

John F. Hannah, senior pastor, New Life Covenant
Church Southeast

"To be in the same space as Pastor McDowell is a real joy. I count it an honor to experience the uniqueness that exudes from his ministry moments. More than a powerhouse in the arena of worship leading and song writing, he is a masterful teacher and presenter of the Word of God. It is abundantly clear that he's devoted his life to ensuring that all come into the awareness of God."

Tasha Cobbs Leonard, GRAMMY Award–winning
worship leader

"In a time when a lot of information contrary to the Word of God is being promoted, this generation needs something more than just traditional church services. This generation needs to see a demonstration of God's power, and this has been found at Deeper Fellowship Church under the guidance of Pastor William McDowell. Miracles, signs and wonders are happening literally every week. These events are providing hope and truth to eliminate any doubt that the God we've heard about is real."

Travis Greene, GRAMMY nominated worship leader;
lead pastor, Forward City Church

"In a world where many are seeking attention, fame and fortune merely for themselves, it never ceases to amaze me to see godly people who are more concerned about God's glory than they are about their own and who still value and desire the presence of God. William McDowell is one of those godly people. You know a tree by the fruit it bears, and there is much fruit in the life and ministry of William McDowell."

Andre Ward, Olympic champion, former world boxing
champion, HBO boxing analyst

"With the humility of a lamb and the glory-filled power of a lion, Pastor William is truly a general of this generation. Not only have I been a firsthand witness to countless miracles under his ministry, but I have also witnessed his personal integrity, passion for God's heart and love for God's people. Out of the clamoring collection of voices in the world that are vying for your attention, Pastor William's voice is one that is proven and worthy to be attended to."

Tony Jones, pastor, Fellowship Church, Winston-Salem,
North Carolina

THE ONLY ANSWER IS
PRAYER

THE ONLY ANSWER IS
PRAYER

AN INTIMATE WALK
WITH GOD INTO
THE MIRACULOUS

WILLIAM McDOWELL,
JASON McMULLEN AND CALEB GRANT

Chosen

a division of Baker Publishing Group
Minneapolis, Minnesota

Published by Chosen Books
11400 Hampshire Avenue South
Bloomington, Minnesota 55438
www.chosenbooks.com

Chosen Books is a division of
Baker Publishing Group, Grand Rapids, Michigan

Printed in the United States of America

Library of Congress Cataloging-in-Publication Data
Names: McDowell, William, 1976- author. | McMullen, Jason, author. | Grant, Caleb, (Pastor), author.
Title: The only answer is prayer : an intimate walk with God into the iraculous / William McDowell, Jason McMullen and Caleb Grant.
Description: Minneapolis, Minnesota : Chosen Books, a division of Baker Publishing Group, [2021] | Includes bibliographical references.
Identifiers: LCCN 2020035714 | ISBN 9780800762094 (trade paper) | ISBN 9780800762278 (casebound) | ISBN 9781493429868 (ebook)
Subjects: LCSH: Prayer—Christianity.
Classification: LCC BV210.3 .M3774 2021 | DDC 248.3/2—dc23
LC record available at https://lccn.loc.gov/2020035714

Cover design by Rob Williams, InsideOut Creative Arts, Inc.

21 22 23 24 25 26 27   7 6 5 4 3 2 1

Contents

Preface

For 21 weeks at Deeper Fellowship, God would not let us leave the subject of prayer. We had been experiencing a move of God, and we sensed that He wanted to prepare our fellowship to see it spread throughout our region and around the world. We knew that if God can do it anywhere, He can do it everywhere. But there has never been a move of God without prayer, and we knew that the healings and miracles had occurred not only because God had chosen for us to see revival but also because of our prayers. God began to tell us that there is more—more miracles, more of His presence—and at the same time, He began to awaken us to another dimension of prayer.

The revelation God poured out challenged and excited us, but more than anything, it changed us. We felt strongly that the word God had spoken to us was not just for Deeper Fellowship, so we adapted our messages into this book.

Pastors Caleb Grant and Jason McMullen and I all contributed to this project. Jason and Caleb are two of my closest friends, and God uses them constantly to deepen my understanding of His Word. This message has been no exception. Unless otherwise noted, I am generally the one talking. But this teaching was developed through much fellowship, study and prayer among the three of us, and it reflects revelations that God gave to all of us.

The unity in which God allowed us to deliver these messages is especially evident in the teaching on the divine council. We unpack this important revelation over the course of three chapters. If we can understand our authority and the access we have been given as sons and daughters of God who are seated with Christ in heavenly places, it will revolutionize our prayer life.

And that is our prayer, our purpose for releasing this book. We want to see you awakened to prayer so that you can experience the life-changing power of an intimate relationship with God. Intimacy is the key to your authority in prayer because when you learn to pray from a place of abiding, your prayer life will radically change. You will see answers to prayer because you will be praying the heart of God.

This is not hype. This is what we have seen happen at Deeper Fellowship. We have seen people move into a new dimension in prayer, and we pray the same will happen for you as you read these pages.

God is inviting us into a deeper relationship. He is inviting us to greater intimacy. He is inviting us into a place of greater authority and agreement with heaven to see the plans and purposes of God become a reality on the earth.

We believe God wants to release a history-making revival that will touch the globe. But God never intended for there to be divine orchestration without human participation. And that human participation is called prayer.

—William McDowell

1

Don't Just Want It—
Pray for It

"I am the true vine, and My Father is the vinedresser.
Every branch in Me that does not bear fruit He takes
away; and every branch that bears fruit He prunes, that
it may bear more fruit."

John 15:1–2 NKJV

My prayer life has gone through many stages. I (Pastor Jason)
used to struggle in prayer, but I no longer struggle. Prayer
used to be a duty, something I would dread, but now it has
become a delight. My hope for you as you read this book is
that prayer would no longer be a duty, an obligatory spiritual discipline, but that it would instead become a delight—
something you want to do.

Why? Because nothing is going to happen in your life apart from prayer.

No move of God has ever happened apart from prayer. Second Chronicles 7:14 (NKJV) says, "If My people who are called by My name will humble themselves, and pray and seek My face, and turn from their wicked ways, then I will hear from heaven, and will forgive their sin and heal their land." Now, in recent days this Scripture has taken on a whole new meaning, but suffice it to say that God responds to prayer! Prayer changes things.

Elijah prayed, and it did not rain for three and a half years. Then he prayed again, and the heavens opened up and rain fell on the land (see James 5:17–18). Daniel prayed, and the answer was such a threat to the enemy that he exerted himself to block it in the heavenlies (see Daniel 10). In Luke 18, Jesus told His disciples a story about a persistent widow to show them that they should never give up in prayer. The apostle Paul tells us in 1 Thessalonians 5 that we should pray without ceasing. This is just a sampling of Scriptures that illustrate the power and importance of prayer.

The Bible makes it clear that prayer is more than important; it is vital. But some believers treat it as something peripheral. They do not treat it as something they should prioritize. That is at least partly because they do not have enough revelation about prayer.

The three of us believe God wants to move His people to another level in prayer. He is calling us to do more than talk about prayer; He is calling us to be *marked* by prayer.

Intercession is not reserved for a select few. It is not supposed to be relegated to a group of old women who meet at church on Thursday nights. We are all called to be intercessors, with Jesus being the Chief Intercessor. The Bible says that Jesus lives to make intercession for us (see Romans 8:34 and Hebrews 7:25). That is what He is doing right now. Please do not miss this: Jesus is our model for everything, including prayer. He never asks us to do something He Himself has not done. He models what He teaches. He is in a posture of prayer for us. And what Jesus is doing, we also are supposed to do. We have been called to pray.

When I look at what is happening in the world around us and wonder what believers can do about it, I am convinced that prayer is the only correct posture for the Church. I am convinced that the only answer is prayer.

Whenever I have been working on my computer for long periods of time, I begin to slouch. (Confession: As I am working on this book, I am doing it.) My wife is good about coming by and lovingly reminding me that my posture is incorrect and that slouching is not good for my back. She helps me remember that if I want to avoid back problems in the future, I need to correct my posture. She loves me. In a similar way, because the Church has been slouching in the place of prayer, we have begun to experience a host of problems because of it. Our slouching looks like slacking, and it is this prayerless posture that is to blame for many of the problems we see in the Church today. We have tried to correct our posture through many other means, but unfortunately there just is no substitute power for a Church on her knees.

The world does not need a Church that is committed to politics; it needs a Church that is committed to prayer. Sometimes I think the Body of Christ has its *P*s wrong. We are worried about playing politics when we need to be concerned about praying. God is looking for a praying Church. He is not looking for a Church that has all the right connections and all the right political positions. He is looking for a Church that will humble itself and pray.

I believe God is calling His people to pray because He is positioning us for the greatest outpouring of His Spirit the world has ever known. We have seen some amazing things at Deeper Fellowship, but I believe God wants to do even greater things here, in your life and in the Body of Christ around the world. But there is a condition. We must pray for it. We have to do more than want God to move in our lives, our families, our nation and the world. We must actively seek Him in prayer.

If you truly want something in the Kingdom of God, you must pray for it. The Bible says, "Ask, and it will be given to you; seek, and you will find; knock, and it will be opened to you" (Matthew 7:7 NKJV). Ask, seek and knock—that is the posture of the believer. We are to be perpetually asking, perpetually seeking and perpetually knocking. We do that in the place of prayer. So if you say you want God to do something in your life, my next question to you is, Are you praying for it? I am not asking if you want it. I am asking if you are praying for it.

It is time to pray. It is time to seek the face of God. It is time to get into position. Why? Because God is about to birth something in the earth, and He needs people who are committed to praying for it to manifest. There is no divine orchestration without human participation.

Confront Yourself

God has something He is trying to get to you. He has a measure of blessing He wants to pour out on you, and He does not want anything to block it, not even you yourself. God does not want you to drown in an ocean of unanswered prayer; He wants you to experience His best and to swim in the sea of fulfillment.

The Bible says, "Hope deferred makes the heart sick" (Proverbs 13:12 NKJV). It is only natural that if your prayers consistently go unanswered, you will begin to wonder if there is a problem. Think of it this way: If you send a text message to someone over and over, and your friend never responds, you start wondering if something is wrong with the relationship. That is kind of how unanswered prayer begins to seem. When you pray to God and begin to wonder why He does not respond, you are doing exactly what God wants you to do. His silence is meant to help you understand that something is wrong, so you will check your relationship with Him.

> **God does not want you to drown in an ocean of unanswered prayer; He wants you to experience His best and to swim in the sea of fulfillment.**

Welcome God's Pruning

Blockages stop the flow of answered prayer, but God has a way of dealing with them. In Scripture, Jesus called this process pruning.

Pruning is the process of removal and refinement. And that is what God wants to do as it relates to your prayer life. He wants to remove the bad theology and bad habits, and refine your passion. God wants to prune your prayer life.

Jesus said,

> "I am the true grapevine, and my Father is the gardener. He cuts off every branch of mine that doesn't produce fruit,

and he prunes the branches that do bear fruit so they will produce even more. You have already been pruned and purified by the message I have given you. Remain in me, and I will remain in you. For a branch cannot produce fruit if it is severed from the vine, and you cannot be fruitful unless you remain in me. Yes, I am the vine; you are the branches. Those who remain in me, and I in them, will produce much fruit. For apart from me you can do nothing."

John 15:1–5

He is the vine; we are the branches. And notice the verse that says, "He cuts off every branch of mine that doesn't produce fruit, and he prunes the branches that do bear fruit so they will produce even more." The pruning process does not stop once you reach a particular level in God. It does not stop once you see a specific prayer answered. No, the pruning process continues, because Jesus is after more fruitfulness. You may say, "Wow, I am producing so much fruit in my life." But Jesus says, "Yes, you are, so I am going to prune you." He does that because He knows you have the potential for more.

As you read this book, God wants to prune your prayer life. He intends to refine you and remove some hindrances to answered prayer so you can produce even more fruit. He does not start by changing your behavior. Why not? Because your life does not start with your behavior. Your life starts with your heart. The Bible says, "Out of the abundance of the heart, the mouth speaks" (Matthew 12:34 NKJV). Where does prayer come from? It comes from the heart. So God knows that if He deals with the heart (the unseen), the seen will take care of itself. Your future is in your heart. Your destiny is in your heart. God wants to circumcise your heart as it relates to your prayer life.

Again, pruning is a process of removal and refinement. I hope you know that all growth is not good growth. A tumor is a growth. I would concede that a tumor that is growing in my body is not good growth. There are a lot of churches that are growing. But not all of that growth is good growth.

The job of the gardener is to remove and refine things so the plants can grow in accordance with his vision for them. That is what God does. He prunes and refines us so we will grow in accordance with His will.

The Master Gardener knows exactly what He wants you to look like, and He shapes you and makes you perfectly symmetrical, perfectly rounded, perfectly fruitful. He shapes you so that you not only look good, but you will also produce the maximum amount of fruit. He is not after growth as much as He is after fruitfulness. In the Body of Christ, we often judge our measure in God by how much we are growing. "I am growing in my faith." "I am growing in my walk."

Great. But the real question is, "Am I being fruitful?"

Reproduction Means You Are Healthy

Fruitfulness means you have the ability to reproduce yourself, and reproduction means you are healthy. Ultimately, God is the opener of wombs. That is why we pray for people struggling with infertility, because we believe God can give life to that womb. When a couple cannot have children, they may go to a doctor to see if there is some level of unhealth in them. When couples struggling to conceive seek out medical assistance, the doctors run diagnostic tests in an attempt to understand how they ended up in that situation. The doctor may conclude that nothing is wrong, but he or she will not know that until the diagnostics have been run.

Just as a doctor will begin to look for signs of unhealth when two people cannot reproduce, so does God when we do not bear fruit. If you want more than growth, if you want to be fruitful, if you want to see revival not just here but everywhere, you must be able to reproduce. And to reproduce, you must become healthy.

But God is still saying, "You need to be pruned." We have seen people get saved, and then God is saying, "Prune them!" We may begin to celebrate because we have seen somebody healed of lupus. But then God breaks in and says, "Prune them!" Why? Because He is not just after growth; He is after fruitfulness—maximum fruitfulness.

God knows your makeup. He knows not only what you have produced but also what you are capable of producing, so He will prune you to the level of your potential. Why? Because He does not want you to miss what He divinely designed you to accomplish. And He always seems to start with your prayer life, because you will never be larger than the size of your prayers. The outcome of your life will never be more fruitful than your prayer life.

God starts with your prayer life because nothing in the Kingdom happens until something is spoken. There are things that God has spoken over you but you have not come into agreement with. How do I know this? Because you say you want it, but you are not praying for it. This is why God, by His Spirit, wants to prune your prayer life so that you will have maximum fruitfulness.

You may not enjoy every minute of the process, but your loving God wants to take your prayer life to a higher level. Are you on board with Him?

Another Dimension

I believe that another level of prayer is getting ready to hit your life and catalyze you into your destiny—that it will literally push you into your destiny.

The apostle Paul wrote, "And the Holy Spirit helps us in our weakness. For example, we do not know what God wants us to pray for. But the Holy Spirit prays for us with groanings that cannot be expressed in words" (Romans 8:26). This verse shows it is not you praying to God; it is God praying through you. This is that other level of prayer—when God prays through you. But in order for Him to do that, you must be pruned so the Holy Spirit can attach Himself to your prayers. The Bible says the Holy Spirit helps us in our weakness. The Greek word translated *helps* in that verse is *synantilambanomai*, and it means "to lay hold along with."[1]

The Holy Spirit wants to make sure that your motives are right, your marriage is right and every other thing is accounted for, because He does not attach Himself to unholiness. He wants your prayer life to be right because He wants to attach Himself to your prayers. And whatever God says through you cannot be stopped. Look at creation. When God spoke, change started happening: The darkness separated from the light, the land separated from the waters, the land produced vegetation and animals, and the seas brought forth sea creatures. Why? Because God spoke. In the dimension of prayer, when we speak out something, it is not us speaking it; it is God. And if God speaks it out, it is going to happen. He says, "Let there be . . . ," and it happens.

Your future is not about striving. Your future is about alignment—aligning your heart. You can be sure that as you align your heart, God is going to attach Himself to your prayers. And as God begins to pray through you and for you, watch out! Things you thought were impossible will begin to happen. Things you thought were held up permanently will begin to manifest themselves after all.

Just think about this. We do not know how to pray. But the Holy Spirit says, "I do!" So He comes alongside you to help you pray. He literally becomes your prayer partner. And the Bible says, "If two of you agree here on earth concerning anything you ask, my Father in heaven will do it for you" (Matthew 18:19). There is no better prayer partner than the Holy Spirit. And if God grabs hold of your prayers, when the Holy Spirit begins to pray His will back to the Father, nothing is going to stop that.

> **We do not know how to pray. But the Holy Spirit says, "I do!" So He comes alongside you to help you pray.**

This kind of Spirit-driven, Spirit-born, Spirit-led prayer is commanded by the apostle Paul, who wrote: "Pray in the Spirit at all times and on every occasion. Stay alert and be persistent in your prayers for all believers everywhere" (Ephesians 6:18). This is the preferred posture for the believer—that we co-labor and cooperate with God in prayer in order to see the fruition of what He wants to happen in the earth.

Through your prayers, God wants to release His plan for the earth. Through your prayers, He wants to release His plans for your life, your family, your city, your nation and even this world. So the question is not, "What do you want God to do?" but rather, "Are you praying for it?"

Do not just stand there wanting it—start praying for it.

Your Prayer Life Is Being Unlocked

For some of us, prayer has not been a delight because we have been trying to do in our own strength what God intended for us to do with His aid. There is no part of the Christian life that you have been called, destined or commanded to live out without the divine enablement of the Holy Spirit, and that includes your prayer life.

Part of why we struggle in prayer is because we do not include our Prayer Partner. But I believe this is part of what is being unlocked in this season—God giving us heavenly assistance and divine enabling to pray as never before.

We talk about the Spirit's enablement when it comes to salvation, the miraculous and healing. It is obvious to us that these things are not possible without the Spirit. But how often do we talk about the enablement of the Spirit when it comes to prayer? In Romans 6:10–11, the Bible tells us that the same Spirit who raised Christ from the dead lives inside of us. He is there, ready to provide heavenly assistance to you and to me so that we can effectively pray the mind and will of God.

The Bible also says we cannot come to Him unless He draws us (see John 6:44). In other words, it is only because of God that you want more of Him. It is because of Him that you desire to do the right thing. In this season as God is unlocking your prayer life, you are going to *desire* to get on your knees and pray in the Spirit. Why? Because He wants to bring some things to birth through you. He wants to bring radical change in your family, in your church, in your city and in your region, and He will do that through your prayers.

Amazingly, God is drawing you into the place of prayer because He wants you to have what He wants for you more than you want it. The way He brings things about on the earth is through the fervent, Spirit-led prayers of His sons and daughters. That includes you.

He is calling you into a deeper place of prayer because He loves you so much that He is not going to let you miss what He has for you.

God Hears and Answers Prayer

Many people get discouraged in prayer because they are not confident that God actually hears them. Or even if they believe that God hears their prayers, they doubt that He will answer them.

If you have ever struggled to believe God hears you and will respond when you pray, remember Romans 8:32: "Since he did not spare even his own Son but gave him up for us all, won't he also give us everything else?"

Additionally, the apostle John shows us in 1 John 5:13–15 that the foundation of our confidence in prayer is our secured future. At first glance, the order we find there is a bit awkward, but I believe that as we labor to look, we will be empowered to see. John is grounding our prayer life in an unshakeable reality. The following understanding should encourage you: If you believe you have eternal life, then you should also believe God hears your prayers and that, because He hears you, He will respond. The lesser is contained in the greater.

If God gave you eternal life, why would He not hear your prayers? If He gave you eternal life, why would He not respond when you pray? If you can believe Him for the ultimate thing—eternal life—why can you not trust Him with your future on earth? If you believe your future in heaven is secure, do not be unsettled about earth. God has given you the ultimate thing, so why would He not give you the lesser thing? If your future in heaven is secure, then your life on earth is settled. God is saying, "Pray to Me about anything, and I am going to respond. Because I have already responded regarding the ultimate thing, you can count on Me for the lesser things."

Sometimes the problem is that we do not know when God will respond, and since we cannot pinpoint when He will answer, we falter in our belief that He will answer at all. This is when we find ourselves worshiping our timeline instead of the Father of time. It is true that we must leave to God the question of "when." But the question of "if" has already been settled. He is going to do it. Do not let not knowing His timing discourage you into prayerlessness.

Have confidence in God. The apostle John wrote that we know He hears us, then we have confidence (see 1 John 5:15). And when we have confidence, we will never stop praying because we know God's desire to respond is based on what He did two thousand years ago. It is not based on the quality of your prayer in the present. It is based on what Jesus did for you two thousand years ago.

As humans, we often start with the lesser and build to the greater. God worked the opposite way. He secured the ultimate thing to give us confidence that He can give us every other lesser thing. We may struggle with the lesser things, but they are based on the greater. So if we do not question the greater thing—our eternal security—that means we should not struggle with the fact that God hears us and will answer our prayers.

Your answer is already in your mouth. Do not stop at wanting it. Pray about it. God hears and will answer your prayers.

PRAYER

Father in heaven, I know that nothing happens apart from prayer. I admit that I have neglected to pray even when I felt impressed to do so. I want to turn a corner and learn anew how to pray. Help me to give prayer top priority in my life. Help me to do more than just read about prayer. Give me the energy and the words so that I can really pray, daily and even hourly. Holy Spirit, You pray the best. Teach me and show me why, what, when, where and how to pray, and keep me going strong. I pray this in the powerful name of Jesus, Amen.

2

Intimacy—The Key to Your Authority

"If you remain in me and my words remain in you, you may ask for anything you want, and it will be granted!"

John 15:7

You have in your mouth the ability to effect change on the earth. If there are things happening in your life, family, church or city that bother you, you have the ability to ask God to do something about them.

There is a particular key to your authority, and it can be found in John 15. Here are Jesus' words again:

"I am the true grapevine, and my Father is the gardener. He cuts off every branch of mine that doesn't produce fruit, and he prunes the branches that do bear fruit so they will produce even more. You have already been pruned and purified by the message I have given you. Remain in me, and I will remain in you. For a branch cannot produce fruit if it is severed from the vine, and you cannot be fruitful unless you remain in me.

"Yes, I am the vine; you are the branches. Those who remain in me, and I in them, will produce much fruit. For apart from me you can do nothing. Anyone who does not remain in me is thrown away like a useless branch and withers. Such branches are gathered into a pile to be burned. But if you remain in me and my words remain in you, you may ask for anything you want, and it will be granted! When you produce much fruit, you are my true disciples. This brings great glory to my Father."

John 15:1–8

Take a close look at verse 7, which appears also at the very beginning of this chapter: "But if you remain in me and my words remain in you, you may ask for anything you want, and it will be granted!" That verse almost seems not to fit, appearing in the middle of a passage about abiding in the vine. (The vine is Jesus Christ.) A lot of people use that verse to say you can get whatever you want from God, as if He is some kind of Santa Claus or a genie in a bottle. But that is not who God is, and that is not what the verse is telling us.

Those people see the words "ask for anything you want," and they miss the key to our authority that is hidden in plain sight. Look at the first part of the verse, which sets up the conditions for asking for anything you want: *"If you remain in me and my words remain in you."*

Intimacy is the key to your authority. When you are intimate with God, you will know what you should ask for because you will be close enough to Him to know what pleases Him.

Let me give you an example of what I (Pastor William) mean. Years ago, my mother went to China. I was probably around twenty, old enough to stay home by myself. But because my mother knew she would be disconnected from me and would not be able to respond quickly if something happened, she left a blank check for me. Her signature on that check gave me access to everything in her bank account in case an emergency arose.

> **Intimacy is the key to your authority. When you are intimate with God, you will know what you should ask for because you will be close enough to Him to know what pleases Him.**

What she gave me with that check was her authority, and because of our relationship she knew she could trust me not to do something crazy with that authority while she was gone. She knew she was not going to come back from China and find that I had gone on a shopping spree or bought a new car. She knew she could trust me with her authority.

Then a number of years later, my car just went kaput, and my mother was going to help me finance a new vehicle. Pastor Jason told me about an auto auction where I could get a car for a better price than at a dealership. So he took me out to the auto auction, and at first we were simply watching the process. It was a feat just to understand the auctioneer, who was talking so fast it sounded like a mixture of English and tongues. It was even harder to keep up with the cars. They were going so fast that if you blinked, the car you wanted could be gone. I mean, within thirty seconds a car could be gone. People were just putting up a hand, and the next thing you knew the car was theirs.

That scared me because I started thinking, *If I just put my hand up and no one else puts their hand up, then that means I have it? What if I don't want it after all?* I am very deliberate in my decision-making; I am not impulsive or hasty at all. But you do not have much time to think at an auto auction, because by the time you think about it, somebody else has bought the car you want. You are forced to know exactly what you are looking for and to make an instantaneous decision.

My mother had sent me to the auction with a certain budget. She said, "You have my authority to spend up to this amount of money." But there was one car I liked, a really good car, and the bid went about five hundred dollars over my budget. Because my mom had given me the authority for only a certain amount, I did not bid any higher. I refused to usurp the authority she had given me. But here is the thing: When I told her about it later, she said, "You know me, and you know that I would have allowed you to have that."

Many of us are walking below the authority God has given us because we are not intimate enough with Him to know how He would want us to use His authority. We do not know what He would say yes to. We are careful about not abusing the authority we have in Christ, but we are not confident enough to push the limits.

The fact is that it is possible to become closer and closer to God. Once you learn the desires of His heart, then you *can* ask for anything and expect it to be done. That is how it works.

God Wants You to Ask, and He Wants to Answer

To really understand what God is saying in John 15, we have to go back to John 13. In that chapter, Jesus was eating with His disciples at the Last Supper. It was the last time He would really talk with them before He was crucified. There Jesus prophesied the betrayal of Judas, knowing that the man who had been walking with Him for three years was about to sell Him out for thirty pieces of silver. And then He foretold Peter's betrayal.

At first Peter objected strenuously, insisting that he would even lay down his life for Him. But Jesus put him in his place: "Let Me tell *you* something. You are going to deny that you even know Me, and you are going to curse the person who says you know Me. In fact, by the time the rooster crows in the morning, you will have denied Me three times."

When we see the famed paintings of the Last Supper, they make us think everyone was sitting around having a nice meal, but that dinner was charged with emotion as soon as Jesus told the disciples that two of them were going to turn their backs on Him—betraying and denying Him.

Jesus was about to die, and He knew it. He was eating with His friends and disciples, with full awareness that the supper would be His last with this band of men. So He had been telling them the things He needed them to know (and that they certainly would never have been able to anticipate). Then He suddenly added, "Oh, by the way, one of you in this room is about to betray Me."

Can you imagine? The twelve men must have been looking around the dimly lit room thinking, *Who in the world could it be? Would one of us do do that?* Probably only some of them heard Him say, "It will be the one who dips bread at the same time as I do." And then Peter spoke up so brashly, and Jesus had to tell him the truth: "Peter, you are going to deny Me, and the rest of you are going to scatter."

That had to have been a somber moment. Or maybe they were up in arms. Either way, it was serious and so heavy that soon Jesus, knowing how much they needed comfort, added, "Don't let your hearts be troubled" (John 14:1).

After everything He had just told them, He comforted them, and then He confirmed His divinity (see verses 6–13). Then He spoke into their future by promising the Holy Spirit (see verse 16). After telling them that He was about to be betrayed and suffer, and that Peter would deny Him and all of them would scatter, and after acknowledging that they had, indeed, been walking with God incarnate for the past three years, Jesus turned and essentially handed each of them (and each of us) a blank check.

> "Just believe that I am in the Father and the Father is in me. Or at least believe because of the work you have seen me do. I tell you the truth, anyone who believes in me will do the same works I have done, and even greater works, because I am going to be with the Father. You can ask for anything in my name, and I will do it, so that the Son can bring glory to the Father."
>
> John 14:11–13

Notice that last line: Answered prayer allows Jesus to bring glory to the Father. He does not want you merely to ask Him. He wants to answer, because only answered prayer brings God glory. This is why Jesus told His disciples, "You can ask for anything in My name, and I will do it, so that I can bring glory to My Father. Yes, ask Me for anything." Jesus went on to explain more to them:

> "I am the true grapevine," He said, "and my Father is the gardener. He cuts off every branch of mine that doesn't produce fruit, and he prunes the branches that do bear fruit so they will produce even more."
>
> John 15:1–2

And then He added,

> "You have already been pruned and purified by the message I have given you. Remain in me [or as some translations put it, "Abide in Me"], and I will remain in you. . . . If you remain in me and my words remain in you, you may ask for anything you want, and it will be granted!"
>
> John 15:3, 7

Jesus' words in John 15 repeat what He said in John 14, in essence: "This is your position of authority; I am giving you a blank check with My name on it. Whatever you pray for will be granted."

Ask for anything. These are powerful words, and they are haunting to me because they force me to examine what I have been asking for, the level at which I have been asking and whether I have been walking in the authority God has given me.

Jesus' promise came with the condition that we first take a certain position. "If ye abide in me" is the way the King James Version renders John 15:7. The word translated *abide* (*menō*) is a verb that can mean to stay in a given place or given state, to continue, to dwell, to endure, to be present or to remain.[1] We do not use the word *abide* much anymore, but it means staying in a certain place, with solid commitment. Jesus is telling us, "I am giving you a blank check with My signature of authority. When you pray with My signature, which is My name, anything you ask will be granted. But there is one vital condition: You must stay close to Me. You must remain there. You must assume a certain posture and not move away."

Another way of saying it is this: *The key to answered prayer is the place from which you ask.*

As followers of Christ, you and I have more authority than we tend to realize, and the authority we have scares the devil.

> **As followers of Christ, you and I have more authority than most of us tend to realize, and the authority we have scares the devil.**

He has devoted himself to operating independently of God and to thwarting whatever builds the Kingdom of God. Can you imagine how the enemy must have felt to hear Jesus say to His disciples, "If you ask anything in My name, I will do it"? And then, "Even though I am leaving the earth, I am going to leave My name here. When you use My name and My authority to ask for anything, I will do it"?

Get this: You and I possess the kind of authority that scares hell. When we operate in our God-given authority, our prayers alone can totally change the affairs of the earth. But that authority is always directly connected to a state of being called *abiding*.

That is why the enemy does everything he can to keep us

from abiding in the Vine (Jesus), where we have been authorized to ask for anything.

How to Stay in Position

Everything in the world is trying to get you out of the position of abiding because the enemy is afraid of your intimacy with God. He does not mind if you shout as long as you are not intimate with God. He does not mind if you get quiet as long as you never get quiet enough to hear from God. He does not mind at all if you dance and get excited about God as long as you do not abide in Him. The enemy is not afraid of whatever you do instead of spending time with God, but he is mortally afraid of your abiding intimacy with Him.

The enemy attacks your relationships, your flesh and your mind. And he does it all for one reason: to get you out of position. Distractions are meant to pull you away from the place of abiding. Relational drama, lost vision, depression and anxiety are all meant to pull you out of your position of authority. Since you cannot ask for anything outside the place of abiding, the enemy uses everything at his disposal to push your buttons so that you will abandon your place of abiding and therefore your place of authority. For example, when you start to have relationship problems, what happens? You tend to lose your focus on God as you fret and fume. No longer are you abiding in peace and joy with Him. Without recognizing what is happening, you have fallen for the enemy's play for your attention. (That does not mean you have lost your place of abiding for good, as you know full well. God's Spirit will draw you back—and the enemy will have lost once more.)

I will say it again: The enemy is scared to death of a believer who is intimate with God. He is scared to death of a believer who knows the heart of God. He is scared to death of a believer who will pray the will of God. He may try to mute the effectiveness of those prayers, but that does not mean he can stop them.

Distractions, gossip, social media, caring too much about what somebody else is doing—these are all things the enemy uses to keep us from paying attention to God. You may find yourself getting into random arguments. You may have gotten up in the morning, had your quiet time and prayed—and then someone called and you ended up in an argument, which left you mad for the rest of the day. The enemy did that to pull you out of the place of abiding. He is messing with your authority, because if he can mess with the authority of the believer, he can roam the earth unchallenged.

The enemy will try anything to distract you, but here are some of the most common ways he attempts to pull you away from the place of intimacy and God-given authority.

Your Relationships

The things that keep happening on your job, the boss that gets on your nerves, the various "haters" who talk about you—these are all distractions to keep you from abiding in the Vine. Do not allow any of it to occupy space in your mind and in so doing to pull you away from abiding in Jesus. When you give attention to haters or troublemakers, you are giving authority to other people; at the least, you are giving them permission to run around in your mind. Settle it: Most of the time, the people you think are against you are not really thinking about you that much. You are thinking about them a lot more than they are thinking about you. They are just distractions. Get back to abiding.

Your Flesh

Uncontrolled living is also a distraction. What is uncontrolled living? It is a nicer way of describing *sin*. You may insist that you have certain urges, that you need to satisfy. But if you are living according to those urges you are living in your flesh, and that means you are living outside of your place of abiding. Jesus has given you the power to put your flesh in subjection (see, for example, 1 Corinthians 9:27). He has given you the power to overcome. It is yours. You no longer have to stay in bondage to your flesh. What makes you think that every believer is so weak that he or she has to sin all the time? You *can* overcome.

Distractions, including sin in particular, will always pull you away from abiding. Pay attention to what is happening. If you wake up in the morning fully determined to give God your day and then a little text ruins your whole day, recognize where that came from—the enemy. That is the way he works, and he does not do that just to steal your peace; he wants to disrupt your authority in Christ.

If you find yourself in the middle of some kind of family conflict, it is not because the enemy just wants to mess with your family relationships; he wants to mess with your authority. He wants to lure you to become so focused on the conflict that you will no longer be able to hear the heartbeat of God. When the enemy attacks your marriage, yes, you should pray about it, but pray about it with this fact in mind: The enemy has targeted you because he is after your place of authority.

Your Mind

Some people have set up such strongholds in their minds they cannot see situations for what they really are. As soon as somebody says "hello," they start wondering what the person's agenda is. That is a stronghold—a fortified, defensive thought pattern—and it needs to be pulled down, because the enemy is using it to mess with their spiritual authority.

How do you know you have a stronghold? If you lash out at a person who tells you the truth about yourself, you have a stronghold. The truth is meant to help you, and you do not want strongholds to stand in the way. Pull them down.

Until you get rid of a stronghold, it is going to keep following you. If you find yourself in the middle of strife on job after job, it is not them; it is you. If every relationship you have ends the same way, it is not them; it is you. Ask God to help you figure yourself out, and submit yourself to Him all over again.

Your Time

The enemy also attacks your time. You say, "Okay, today, I am going to spend time with God. Here I am, off work and with plenty of free time. He is going to have my whole day. Jesus, it is just going to be me and You. Coffee with Jesus." Then somewhere around five or six that evening you realize, *I just don't know where the day went.* The enemy has attacked your time to keep you from abiding in Jesus.

Your Health

Did you know that when the enemy attacks your health, what he is really after is your authority in Christ? I know a lot of people do not see it that way. They do not want to see demons hiding behind every bush, and rightly so. But just because every ailment is not directly caused by a demon does not mean some health issues are not an attack of the enemy.

Recently, I hurt my hand badly and needed surgery. I could not drive or button my shirts, and my wife had to cut up my food as if I were a toddler. I got frustrated with it. For a long time I kept wondering, "Why did this happen? I have so much to do—in fact, too much to do. Here I am, canceling trips, but I need to do this and this and this. . . ." And then I realized that what I really needed was to rest. After I figured out that God wanted me to rest, I started using my time to write new songs.

The enemy always wants to keep you from the place of abiding in Him. And a negative health report can definitely get your focus on your health and off abiding in Him. Never forget that Jesus gave us the promise of healing, thus proving that He is the Lord over all, including sickness.

Your Wealth

The enemy will attack your finances, and one of his tactics is to try to woo you away from abiding in Jesus by using the allure of the world.

Americans are some of the richest people on planet earth, and yet most of us are not satisfied with our money. We like to say we have "more month than money," but compared with other parts of the world, we are truly wealthy. The enemy wants us to replace our pursuit of God with the pursuit of money.

He wants us to be dissatisfied with what God has provided. He wants us to compare ourselves to others and to compete with them. He wants us to exhaust ourselves with our striving to acquire more wealth. He wants to make us deaf and blind to what the Lord Jesus told us:

> "Don't store up treasures here on earth, where moths eat them and rust destroys them, and where thieves break in and steal. Store your treasures in heaven, where moths and rust cannot destroy, and thieves do not break in and steal. Wherever your treasure is, there the desires of your heart will also be.
>
> "No one can serve two masters. For you will hate one and love the other; you will be devoted to one and despise the other. You cannot serve God and be enslaved to money."
>
> Matthew 6:19–21, 24

The Allure of Fame

The enemy will use the allure of fame to distract you from abiding. Many people are so hungry to be famous that they are willing to look like a fool to do so. They will do anything for fifteen seconds of popularity. (We used to say people were looking for "fifteen minutes of fame," but nobody is looking at anyone that long anymore.) The allure of fame will pull you away from abiding in Christ. Success leads to self-glorification—and it is intended to pull you away from that place of abiding.

I have spent so long describing these distractions and attacks because I want you to be aware of the lengths the enemy will go to. He is so afraid of people who pursue intimacy with God that he will throw everything into their path in order to pull them away from abiding.

The enemy wants you to forget about the power of abiding in Jesus. He does not want you to notice how he keeps working to pull you away from the place of your authority. He does not want you to look at your life circumstances with clear vision so that you can declare, "I am not going there. I am not having that conversation. I am not going to do that. I am okay with my salary. I am okay with my house. I am okay with my car because I have peace, and that peace comes from my intimacy with God. I am not going to get into a rat race and lose my authority."

You do not have to be a millionaire to change the world. You do have to be willing to abide.

When you abide in Christ, your prayers can change the world. Can you imagine seeing the rates of crime and homelessness plummet in your city simply because you (having chosen intimacy with God over everything else) asked the Lord to send revival to your city? Can you imagine prostitutes turning their lives over to Jesus, intractable diseases being healed and lives being restored purely because you chose to abide? Well, it can happen where you live! It is happening here at Deeper Fellowship, and it is happening in other parts of the country and around the world.

There are churches housed in the same strip malls with strip joints and gun shops that are seeing lives changed because they understand their authority. Let the reign of the Kingdom of God be established here on earth. Let God's heart be established in you. Today, the Lord is after a group of people who will no longer be distracted by the attacks of the enemy. He wants to teach you how to increase your awareness of your authority—and how to abide in Him.

Strategies for Abiding

God wants to position us with His authority, so that we can "pray His heart." Because of our abiding in Christ Jesus, we believers can participate in the establishment of the plan of God on the earth. I want to be part of that, and I am sure you do, too.

In order to do so, we must take to heart what Scripture says:

> Do not love this world nor the things it offers you, for when you love the world, you do not have the love of the Father in you. For the world offers only a craving for physical pleasure, a craving for everything we see, and pride in our achievements and possessions. These are not from the Father, but are from this world. And this world is fading away, along with everything that people crave. But anyone who does what pleases God will live forever.
>
> 1 John 2:15–17

We are sons of God, and our Father has given us His perspective in the Old Testament as well as the New:

> For the Lord declares, "I have placed my chosen king on the throne in Jerusalem, on my holy mountain." The king proclaims the Lord's decree: "The Lord said to me, 'You are my son. Today I have become your Father. Only ask, and I will give you the nations as your inheritance, the whole earth as your possession. You will break them with an iron rod and smash them like clay pots.'"
>
> Psalm 2:6–9

Look at how the Passion Translation puts the same verses:

"I myself have poured out my King on Zion, my holy mountain. I will reveal the eternal purpose of God. For he has decreed over me, 'You are my favored Son. And as your Father I have crowned you as my King Eternal. Today I became your Father. Ask me to give you the nations and I will do it, and they shall become your legacy. Your domain will stretch to the ends of the earth. And you will shepherd them with unlimited authority, crushing their rebellion as an iron rod smashes jars of clay!'"

We remember that Jesus said to His disciples, "Ask Me for anything." And here in Psalm 2, He says, "Ask me to give you the nations, and I will do it." At first, you may respond, "Okay, He wants us to ask for nations." Yes, but there is something more important to see here. Yes, you can ask for big things from God, but in Psalm 2 God is inviting David to pray His heart into the earth. By saying, "Ask for the nations," He is saying, "Ask for the rule of God." And when David, who was intimate with God, participated in this kind of prayer, God answered by giving us Christ.

The enemy wants to keep you praying for small stuff. He wants you to be preoccupied with praying about your bills because he does not want you to pray that revival will break forth in your city. But you can trust that God is drawing you to Himself for bigger purposes. His words will not fall to the ground and neither will your prayers. In fact, even when you die, your prayers will remain.

God is looking for people—a group of people—who are intimate enough with Him to understand His heart. Their prayers will outlive them. Our children and our children's children are going to walk in revival if that is what we pray for. Because we abide with God, we can see the future ahead of time and proclaim it now.

God did not tell us a revival was coming to Orlando. He said, "I am sending a global revival." We are seeing it here because we started praying for it to come here. We started to claim it. And God responded by saying, "I am not just going to answer this prayer by sending revival to a distant land. I am going to put the answer in your midst."

In Orlando, Florida, I (Pastor William) am amazed to hear so many people talking about revival. I love it. God started speaking to us about revival in 2011. Before hundreds of people started crowding into our building, we were talking about seeing a move of God that would not only affect the city, but also the globe. As God spoke, I started writing songs about what was coming. One of them is called "Expecting." The words are simple and pure, but powerful: "I'm expecting. Anticipating. A move of God."[2]

We will never be satisfied until heaven invades our lives. We are praying to see blind eyes opened, and we are seeing it happen. We are praying to see cities and regions change, and I believe we will see it—because we have been praying for it, and we have been longing for it. With all our hearts, we believe that we will see a move of God, and we have declared prophetically that change is coming.

When I spend time with God to write music, I ask God to show me the future. I want the declarations I write to be in the mouths of other believers so the future can be attracted to the present. In music-recording cycles, you have to record in one season and release it in another. So to be relevant, you need to know what the next season holds.

In 2016, I released a record called *Sounds of Revival*, which was the soundtrack of what we believed we were going to see. And then one year later, we felt that God was saying, "So you want to see that? I am going to bring revival in the earth, but I will prove it by bringing revival among you and in you and around you. I am going to let you see it." And that is what is happening now. He works that way to demonstrate to us that those who abide in Him have the authority to declare and release things into the earth that not only affect the earth at large but also right where they live.

David received the blessing of his prayers, and so do we. David's blessing was that his kingdom would be established forever. How could his kingdom and his throne be established forever if he himself did not live forever? It could happen because the legacy of his prayer would live on; Jesus' coming made David's kingdom an eternal one.

Psalm 2:8 says, "Ask of Me, and I will give You the nations for Your inheritance" (NKJV). And remember what John 15:7 tells us: "But if you remain in me and my words remain in you, you may ask for anything you want, and it will be granted!"

What have you been praying for? I do not know where the quote originated, but I once heard Brian Houston of Hillsong Church say, "If God were to answer all of your prayers, would it change the world or change you?" That is one of the ways you can actually identify how large your prayer life is: Can it change the world or only you?

Stay in Position

When Jesus said, "You may ask for anything in My name, and I'll do it," He was not promising to gratify your every whim. As long as a believer is seeking God's will in his or her life, Jesus will grant every request that will help to bring about this result. When your prayers are guided (even dominated) by the goal of serving the Kingdom of God, you can be absolutely sure that every one of your prayers will be answered.

Since answered prayer is connected to our position in Christ, how can we learn how to remain securely in a position of abiding? There are three primary ways:

1. Be satisfied with Him.

I know it sounds simple. But do you know one of the reasons Christians spend so much time on social media? It is because they are not satisfied with Him. They actually get a dopamine high every time somebody likes one of their posts, and they go back to see how many people liked their posts because they need that gratification. It shows that they are not satisfied enough with God.

Being satisfied with God is all-important for anybody who wants to be used by Him. You can know if you are slipping away from the Vine if you start to find that you are aiming for the approval and the applause of others. Be satisfied with Him alone, and everything will fall into place.

I am not talking only about church people, because they are conditioned to respond a certain way. But what if you have to speak the truth at your job? There will not be anyone there to say, "That's good." Nobody is going to be applauding you when you say, "You probably shouldn't sleep with her."

Nobody is going to stand there saying, "Preach it!" when the evangelism team goes out on the street and they come up to a drug addict and say, "You don't have to stay this way. There is hope for you. You don't have to try to alter your mental state because of your pain. Jesus knows where you are, and He can heal you and set you free." Nor when they give their lives to Jesus on the street will anyone be there to play an organ or sing a song. When you go home, you are going to have to be satisfied with Jesus saying, "I am proud of you today."

You know what I am talking about. When you minister in some way, something inside you wants to hear everyone say, "That was awesome!" But what does it matter if everybody around you tells you that your preaching was awesome but *He* does not? Just flip on the TV, and you will see people preaching all kinds of stuff that is not in the Bible while the audience gets up on their feet talking about how amazing their words were. I wonder what the Lord thinks about that kind of error, of using the Word to manipulate people to send in money?

Be satisfied with Him alone. Jesus said, "I am the bread of life. Whoever comes to me will never be hungry again. Whoever believes in me will never be thirsty" (John 6:35). I love the way it reads in the Passion Translation: "I am the Bread of Life. *Come every day to me and you will never be hungry.* Believe in me and you will never be thirsty" (emphasis added).

Be satisfied with Jesus. This is how you abide, because if you are not satisfied with Him, instead of staying in the place of abiding, you will continually be leaving it to find satisfaction.[3]

Be satisfied with *Him.* That is all.

2. Recognize your need for Him.

Being dependent on God is not weakness; it is maturity. The old folks used to say they were leaning on the Father's everlasting arms, safe and secure. That is the posture we are to take with God. Always remember what Jesus said: "Yes, I am the vine; you are the branches. Those who remain in me, and I in them, will produce much fruit. For apart from me you can do nothing" (John 15:5).

3. Cherish His words.

Going deeper into Jesus' vine metaphor, we discover that the Word is what flows between the vine and the branches. We can see it in the words of Jesus: "But if you remain in me *and my words remain in you*, you may ask for anything you want, and it will be granted!" (John 15:7, emphasis added).

You can reach a level of intimacy that is characterized by such a love of God's words that the only words you pray are His words. Such intimacy with the heart of God causes you to pray exactly what He wants. This is a crucial thing. Many people look at John 15:7 and think it means we can pray for what *we* want. But God is not a genie in a bottle. When you want what He wants and pray it, what you are seeking will come to pass.

This puts us in a place of authority. It is as if we have been given a blank check (signed by Jesus) for things that can be drawn from His account to bring glory to the Father.

Together, you and I have so much authority, individually and collectively, that our prayers ought to be affecting the region where we live in noticeable ways. You should not have to run for mayor to change your city, because your city will be affected already by what you pray. The devil does not have the blank check—you do. The enemy of God should never be allowed to do whatever he wants in the region where you live.

The devil is fighting what should be a losing battle to pull us believers away from our place of abiding. He wants us to be distracted from praying with authority. He wants us to spend all of our time and energy praying for less than what God intends us to pray about. Remember that Jesus said He knows what you need before you ask. He wanted to assure you of that so you could turn your attention to bigger things:

When you pray for revival, God sends it.

When you pray from the place of abiding, God answers.

PRAYER

Lord, I did not know about the extent of my authority in prayer. Now that I have learned more about it, help me to wield it faithfully and effectively. Keep me humble and surrendered to Your will and keep me from wavering or giving up. Teach me what "ask for anything in My name" means for my prayer life today. Please guard me from distractions. Above all, help me to abide in You, this day and always. Because of Jesus, Amen.

3

Prayer—
The Language of Faith

Then Jesus said to the disciples, "Have faith in God. I tell you the truth, you can say to this mountain, 'May you be lifted up and thrown into the sea,' and it will happen. But you must really believe it will happen and have no doubt in your heart. I tell you, you can pray for anything, and if you believe that you've received it, it will be yours."

Mark 11:22–24

Every God-inspired revival that has ever happened—whether 150 years ago or in the recent past—has been the result of prayer. Whenever revival spreads like wildfire across the globe, it is because men and women dared to pray the Holy Spirit down from above.

We must be motivated to pray because, among other benefits, prayer puts us in a position to lay claim to the promises of God. This is an important key because too many people operate in passive faith, standing on the sidelines, hoping something will magically happen one day. In fact, one big reason many Christians do not see the fulfillment of what God has said about them is that they do not pray it through. Passive faith is the kind that believes, but folds its hands in its lap and waits, while active faith believes and raises its hands, praying *until*.

Make no mistake: Without prayer, we will never experience the fulfillment of what God has promised. And we will not see the answers to our prayers without faith.

The Necessity of Faith

Faith means believing God and trusting Him wholeheartedly. By believing Him, we position ourselves to receive all that He has spoken prophetically about us. As Pastor Bill Johnson of Bethel Church once said, prophecy comes to make us hungry. Just knowing that God has a word for His people should make us want to seek His face even more. Prophecy, however, is not supposed to help us strategize or figure out how to make a thing happen in our own strength. Prophecy must be coupled with faith. Active, trusting, obedient faith is an absolute necessity.

What God wants to do in your life and in mine is so big and so massive that nothing we do apart from having faith in Him will ever bring it to pass. When we receive a word from the Lord, we get a picture of the future, a picture that should inspire us to pursue Jesus wholeheartedly. Then no crisis or obstacle should be able to thwart the plan of God; this is because of the insatiable hunger we have for Him, and the fervent prayers stirred up by that hunger.

In Mark 11, Jesus teaches the disciples about the necessity of faith:

> Now the next day, when they had come out from Bethany, He was hungry. And seeing from afar a fig tree having leaves, He went to see if perhaps He would find something on it. When He came to it, He found nothing but leaves, for it was not the season for figs. In response Jesus said to it, "Let no one eat fruit from you ever again." And His disciples heard it.
>
> Verses 12–14 NKJV

In this passage of Scripture, Jesus approached the tree, but when He saw it had no fruit for Him to eat, He cursed it. His actions seem perplexing because the passage declares that it was not actually the season for figs. Why, then, would Jesus have expected to find any fruit on that tree? Because it had leaves. If you know anything about fig trees, you know the leaves and the figs blossom at the same time. It might not have been the right season for figs, but the tree at first glance appeared to be bearing fruit, because it was leafed out. The tree was saying, "Hey, look at me; I have leaves." It was trying to fool people with its appearance, when in reality it had no fruit on it. So Jesus cursed the tree and moved on.

The next day, it happened that He and the disciples walked past the fig tree again. Jesus did not even stop to give them an object lesson, but Peter noticed the dried-up tree. Only the day before, it had been green and leafy. He could not resist speaking up: "And Peter calling to remembrance saith unto him, Master, behold, the fig tree which thou cursedst is withered away. And Jesus answering saith unto them, Have faith in God" (Mark 11:21–22 KJV).

Peter was no doubt shocked at how fast the word of the Lord had come to pass. He probably thought it would take days or even months for the tree to dry up. At the longest, he probably thought it would not fully die off until at least the following year.

Peter and the other disciples did not understand much yet. Even though they had been walking with Jesus every day, watching Him perform miracles, they had yet to develop their faith in Jesus. Their faith needed to be enlarged in every way. They had been following Him faithfully, having abandoned their homes and livelihoods. They were not halfhearted disciples. These men had witnessed the miracle at the wedding when Jesus turned the water into fine wine. They had been beside Him when He healed the blind man and the paralyzed man at the pool of Bethesda. They had even had a front-row seat at the feeding of the five thousand in the wilderness. And yet they still had limited expectations. In this case, it does not appear that they really believed the tree would die, even though that is exactly what Jesus had decreed. In some ways, they were like the figless fig tree: Just as the tree appeared to have figs, so they appeared to have faith. But their reactions said otherwise.

Jesus, knowing all things, could have told His mystified disciples, "You see, I have complete authority, and when I speak to creation, it has to respond." But He did not elaborate. He simply said, "Have faith in God."

The Object of Our Faith

To see something miraculous take place in your life, you must have faith in God. You cannot have faith in God if you do not know Him. Therefore, your level of faith will be connected directly to the level of revelation you have of God. That is why Paul said in 2 Timothy 1:12 (NKJV), "I know whom I have believed," when he was in the middle of testifying about the depth of his relationship with God:

> For God has not given us a spirit of fear, but of power and of love and of a sound mind. Therefore do not be ashamed of the testimony of our Lord, nor of me His prisoner, but share with me in the sufferings for the gospel according to the power of God, who has saved us and called us with a holy calling, not according to our works, but according to His own purpose and grace which was given to us in Christ Jesus before time began, but has now been revealed by the appearing of our Savior Jesus Christ, who has abolished death and brought life and immortality to light through the gospel, to which I was appointed a preacher, an apostle, and a teacher of the Gentiles. For this reason I also suffer these things; nevertheless I am not ashamed, for *I know whom I have believed* and am persuaded that He is able to keep what I have committed to Him until that Day.
>
> 2 Timothy 1:7–12 NKJV, emphasis added

Paul is saying, "I *know* the One I believe. My faith is strong. I can go through this because I know *Him*. I can believe for this because—and only because—I know Him."

One of the biggest reasons Christians struggle in their walk with the Lord is they do not really know Him. Yes, they know Him on a surface level, but there is no real sense of closeness or intimacy with Him. As a result, they do not realize what a generous gift faith is to the believer, and they take it for granted. When they hear the words "Have faith in God," they may think, *Yeah, okay. "Have faith in God." Got it.* To them, it seems like a simple Sunday school lesson, but it is not. Faith is our solid foundation!

Why is faith in God so important? Because the object of our faith is God Himself. Faith all by itself has no object, and therefore it has no value. Jesus underscored this point when He told the disciples to have faith *in God.* Jesus never said to have faith in faith or have faith in oneself. The Bible says, "Without faith it is impossible to please him: for he that cometh to God must believe that he is, and that he is a rewarder of them that diligently seek him" (Hebrews 11:6 KJV). Faith in someone or something other than God displeases God and keeps us away from Him. Our faith *in God* is the secret to walking in divine, supernatural power.

Slogans such as "Just Believe" or "Have Faith" are nice sayings to put on a T-shirt, but they are meaningless, just as having faith in the universe is meaningless. Only when God—who is omnipotent—is the object of our faith do we have the power we need to live a victorious life. Without that faith, we are operating in our own strength only. When people say they have faith, what they are trying to do, including some Christians, is to *will* something into existence by means of positive thinking and imagination. That is New Age mysticism, and believers need to be careful not to be fooled by such false teaching.

Too often, people who come to the altar for special prayer try their best to make something happen in their own strength. They may profess, "I believe; I have faith." But in what or whom do they believe? If they do not truly believe that God is going to act, then who is going to answer their prayers? The person laying hands on them has no authority to answer prayer. A person can spend all day at the altar, but if he or she does not believe God is present, or if the object of their faith is faith itself, they will leave the altar the same way they came.

Childlike Faith

There is a correct way to get what you need from God: Every time you pray, pray with the assurance that God can do it. You may not know how He is going to do it, but all He asked you to do is believe in Him. It is quite simple. Many people will begin to see miraculous results if they get back to a more childlike faith. The Scripture says signs and wonders shall follow those who believe (see Mark 16:17). It does not say signs and wonders will follow those who preach and hold miracle crusades. It does not say signs and wonders will follow those who have been given the gift of healing. It says signs and wonders will follow those who believe. If you have the faith of a child when you pray, you will see God answer your prayers.

When you have kids, they believe you can do anything. My (Pastor Caleb's) son believes I can make myself invisible. He actually believes I am invisible when he cannot see me and he does not know I am hiding. He turns away and I disappear. "Wow! Dad is invisible!" But I am standing right there the entire time, just out of his sight.

Why do our children believe we can do anything, yet we do not believe our Father God can do anything? The reason is simple enough: As we get older, we allow cynicism and skepticism to overtake us. We forget our history with God, the many experiences we have had while walking with Him. You know it was God who healed your body last year, so now why do you not believe He can heal you again? You remember how God took care of your rent and put food on your table that time when you lost your job, but now you are worried that a bill collector is calling you?

God is the One who sent those blessings. Never forget how good He is. Put your complete faith in Him. He will never disappoint you.

The Purpose of Faith

Okay, we understand that God must be the object of our faith. But our faith also has a personal purpose, which is to remove the mountains that keep us from fulfilling our prophetic destiny.

"Mountain" is a metaphor for an obstacle or something that is perceived to be big and immoveable. A negative report, a failing marriage, uncontrolled debt—these are all mountains. And there is one more thing that we tend not to see as a mountain: our response to prophetic words about our destiny. After they receive a prophetic word, some people let doubt take over. Before they know it, they have become paralyzed with fear that what God has said will never come to pass. Fear is the opposite of faith. Fear does not come from above; it is demonic and tormenting. It presents a big obstacle, indeed a mountain.

Next time you come face-to-face with a mountain in your life, remember what Jesus told the disciples when they saw the withered fig tree: "Have faith in God" (Mark 11:22). In that place, He went on to explain to the disciples (and to us) how to get rid of a mountain by simply believing:

> For verily I say unto you, That whosoever shall say unto this mountain, Be thou removed, and be thou cast into the sea; and shall not doubt in his heart, but shall believe that those things which he saith shall come to pass; he shall have whatsoever he saith.
>
> Mark 11:23 KJV

If a mountain in your life is obstructing your view of God, you should realize that your perception of Him is wrong. There you are, thinking that the thing is bigger than God or equal to Him. Genesis 18:14 says, "Is anything too hard for the LORD?" Do we not think that God can handle it? It is similar to the way someone hopes that the doctor will not mention the C-word, thinking, *If it's cancer, I don't know how God is going to do it.* Then when the doctor says, "It's just an infection that can be treated with antibiotics," the person is relieved: *Whew, close call.*

But even if the doctor had said it was cancer, would it not have been just as easy for God to heal cancer as it would have been for Him to heal an infection? Nothing, absolutely nothing, is so difficult for God that He would have to get up off His throne in order to muster extra strength. And you do not have to pray any longer or work any harder to get Him to answer your prayers. In any case, your faith is not in the words you say; your faith is in the all-powerful, loving God Himself. There is no one like the Lord, and nothing is too hard for Him.

When I pray for the sick, I do not know how God is going to heal the people, but I know He is a healer. Overnight, He healed someone in our church who had been stricken with a fatal brain-eating amoeba. I do not know how He healed her, but He did it. I do not know how a sister who had been paralyzed for two years after having a stroke was back up on her feet and jumping within two days. I do not know how a baby who had been partially brain-dead was suddenly able to do what the doctor said she would never do. I do not know how He healed one woman of lupus in the blink of an eye, but she is healed. I do not know how He has made tumors disappear, but He has done it. It is not my job to figure out how. It is not my job to figure out when. It is my job to have faith—in Him!

No wonder Zechariah, after he prophesied, "Not by might, nor by power, but by my spirit, saith the LORD of hosts," then said, "Who art thou, O great mountain? before Zerubbabel thou shalt become a plain" (Zechariah 4:6–7 KJV). In essence, Zechariah was saying, "I know who my God is, so who are you in comparison to Him, O great mountain?" It never matters how overwhelming the circumstances are that you are facing; God is always going to be bigger than any mountain you will ever confront.

Do Not Scoff at Prophecies

Did you know that faith has an enemy? Actually, it has many enemies, but what I am talking about is what the apostle Paul calls scoffing, which means mocking and doubting. "Do not scoff at prophecies," he wrote to the church in Thessalonica:

Always be joyful. Never stop praying. Be thankful in all circumstances, for this is God's will for you who belong to Christ Jesus. Do not stifle the Holy Spirit. Do not scoff at prophecies.

1 Thessalonians 5:16–20

Often when Christians read this passage of Scripture, they tend to zero in on verse 18: "Be thankful in all circumstances." That is all right, because we absolutely should give thanks; in fact, thankfulness is the gateway to God's presence (see Psalm 100:4). But the other part of the passage, "Do not scoff at prophecies," is also important to pay attention to. When they hear a prophetic word, some people get busy trying to bring it to pass, but others just scoff at it. As a result, they fail to surrender to the perfect timing of God.

You would think that we would enjoy hearing prophecy more than that. After all, it is exciting. Why should there be a need for the apostle Paul to write, "Do not scoff at prophecies"?

Think about how prophecies are usually received. When a pastor or visiting evangelist calls a person to the front so that he or she can give that person a word from the Lord, everyone's faith increases in anticipation of what is about to be said. I think it has to do with where many of us place our faith—in our own abilities to perform a word from the Lord. As we listen to the word being delivered, we start to calculate what it will take to fulfill it.

In a typical scenario, the Holy Spirit invades the church and the entire congregation experiences new levels of faith. I have seen this happen many times in our church. But inevitably, some of the excitement comes from the fact that the people may feel they can accomplish the prophetic word in their own strength. That can be exciting to anticipate. But when the fulfillment of a prophecy is obviously beyond their ability to bring about, they can suddenly become suspicious of it, thinking or even saying, "That word is just too much." Do you know what happens next in their hearts? Scoffing.

Paul knew that the Christians in Thessalonica would face that kind of a challenge. The Thessalonian church was a "happening church." It was a young body of believers, and God was moving in their midst, revealing Himself in powerful ways. Nevertheless, here we see that Paul was compelled to tell the Thessalonians in the final admonition of his letter not to scoff at, or mock, prophetic words. I think He wanted them to know that in the coming days, the prophecies would seem so unbelievable that their natural inclination would be to scoff by saying, "Yeah, right. Who, us?" Paul wanted to warn the new believers not to doubt what God was going to do with them.

This is easy to fall into, as I know from personal experience. There are things God has said about my future that are so big I cannot wrap my mind around them. At first I am excited: "Yes!" But after a time, I begin to reconsider: "Well, we will have to see how that works out. . . ." You may have had the same experience. At first you have received a prophetic word with joy, saying, "Yes, God. This is awesome! Thank You, Jesus!" But the joy was short-lived once you started asking yourself, "How is it going to happen? This sounds impossible."

Have you ever responded to a prophecy with just an "Okay, if You say so, God"? We may characterize our halfhearted response as humility, but really it shows a lack of faith. That is not the same as agreeing with God about those things He has spoken over your life. We need to agree with God whole-heartedly about the things He speaks both privately and publicly over our lives. Although we Christians do not like to admit that we do not agree with God, that may be exactly what we are doing. It can be different if God tells me I am going to do something for Him that does not require much faith; I will probably get excited, even overjoyed. But when the thing is beyond my control and ability and imagination, my initial response quickly cools down to just an "Okay," which amounts to a form of scoffing.

Another way we scoff at a prophetic word is to give God a list of questions: *Do You know how old I am? Do You know how young I am? Do You know what I have been through? Do You know how limited my resources are?*

What? Do you think He does not know? He knows every-thing, and He is all-powerful. Is He not more than sufficient to see His word through to fulfillment?

When God called me to plant Deeper Fellowship Church, He had blessed me in that season financially so that I had enough to finance the vision initially. It took a massive step of faith to release that amount of money. But then God called me to do something next in ministry that was far beyond my financial ability. He stepped up my call. Now my own finances would no longer suffice. My response was not as eager as it had been the first time. In retrospect, I can see that I was scoffing. To my limited understanding, I could not see at all how it would work out.

But I definitely needed God's help in order to pursue the next part of the vision He had shown me. I needed a lot more faith.

I got married, and the Lord told me to let go of the business I owned so that I could reduce my expenses. At the time, it all made sense to me because my expenses were more or less killing me. But where would the money come from? I said to Him, "God, this does *not* make sense because when I could not afford it, You were telling me to run the business, and now that I can afford it, You are telling me to let it go."

What I failed to recognize was that my obedience would unlock other resources to me. Right when the Lord told me to reduce my expenses by eliminating the business, He increased my financial blessing. In the natural, it did not fully make sense to me. I had struggled financially when I had the business, but when I let the business go, floodgates of resources opened up.

I did not understand that part of my preparation for the next thing was being forced to step into a new level of faith. Had I kept the business, I would not have had access to the outside resources that would help fund the new work He was calling me to.

That helped me learn that scoffing is nothing more than unbelief dressed up in church clothes. I could see that scoffing is the reason many Christians miss out on the blessings and favor of God. But more importantly, I came to understand that scoffing is sin because unbelief is sin, according to the writer of the book of Hebrews:

> Be careful then, dear brothers and sisters. Make sure that your own hearts are not evil and unbelieving, turning you away from the living God. You must warn each other every day, while it is still "today," so that none of you will be deceived by sin and hardened against God. For if we are faithful

to the end, trusting God just as firmly as when we first believed, we will share in all that belongs to Christ. Remember what it says: "Today when you hear his voice, don't harden your hearts as Israel did when they rebelled."

Hebrews 3:12–15

If you have been a scoffer, repent and ask the Holy Spirit to give you the mind of Christ.

Ask in Faith

If you want to walk supernaturally and pray effectually, you must understand that God operates completely outside your reach. If He worked within the realm of what you could do, *you* would be God. He wants you to know He is the God who can do "exceedingly abundantly above all that we ask or think, according to the power that works in us" (Ephesians 3:20 NKJV). But He wants you to *ask*.

Jesus told us, "Therefore I say unto you, What things soever ye desire, when ye pray, believe that ye receive them, and ye shall have them" (Mark 11:24 KJV). There it is in black and white, and yet some Christians are still too afraid to make their requests known to the Lord. Let's be honest, though. We would never admit that we think or believe God cannot do something. Most of us would never allow the words, "I do not believe God" to come out of our mouths. We would be ashamed to call ourselves a Christian if we said that. But whether we say it or not, what we truly believe becomes evident in the fact that we will not ask. We tend not to ask for things we do not believe can happen.

Which brings us back to prayer.

Get this: A faith that believes is a faith that prays and does not doubt. Our words do not move God—faith does.

When you pray, do not waste time wondering *if* it can be done. Step up with full confidence that whatever you ask and believe, you will receive. (I did not make up that statement; it comes from the Scripture I just quoted—Mark 11:24.)

Get this: A faith that believes is a faith that prays and does not doubt. Our words do not move God—faith does.

Keep this Scripture in mind. And stop throwing things into the prayer pot that do not need to be there; they only make your faith cloudy. We muddy the waters of prayer by asking *how* and *when*, and by saying, "*If* it is Your will, God." Such words can ruin the power and simplicity of prayer, and they make people question whether or not God is omnipotent.

In praying for the sick, go back to this simple way of praying. Every time you pray, pray with the assurance that He *can*. You may wonder how He will, but all He asked you to do is believe that He can. Do not let your mind get in the way of your miracle. Many people would begin to see miraculous results if they would get back to childlike faith.

We must leave no room for doubt, because other people's lives hang in the balance. I (Pastor William) travel often, and my favorite testimonies are not just the miracles that happen instantly. Of course I love those. But I also love it when I go back to a city, and someone runs up to me and says, "Oh my goodness! I can't believe I'm seeing you. You prophesied to me four years ago that this would happen and that would happen, and guess what? All of it did."

To which I say, "Thank You, Jesus." Those people experienced a number of miraculous events because I (and they) did not question if God could do it. We had faith in Him. We *knew* He would.

A Faith That Prays

Theologian Kevin DeYoung said, "Prayerlessness is an expression of our meager confidence in God's ability to provide and of our strong confidence in our ability to take care of ourselves without God's help." He goes on to say, "A heart that never talks to God is the heart that trusts in itself." Simply put, "prayerlessness is unbelief."[1]

Prayerlessness—please get this—is not fundamentally a discipline problem. At its core, it is a faith problem. Most of the time when we hear messages about prayer, we think to ourselves, *I need to pray more. I need to become more disciplined. Tomorrow morning, that's it; I am going to get up thirty minutes early and pray.* Even if we follow through, we soon bog down and start laboring in prayer. You must realize that if you find yourself laboring in prayer, you actually have a faith issue.

We in the United States may wonder why the African continent experiences so many miracles. It is because of their faith in God, their faith that prays. I wish every North American Christian could witness a prayer meeting in action in one of the countries of Africa. Then they would know why the believers in Africa experience so many miracles. Significant prayer results come from significant faith—and those believers *believe.*

This is nothing new, but we tend to forget it. Centuries ago, John Calvin knew the benefit of talking with God. He said prayer is "the chief exercise of faith."[2] Modern author

Jon Bloom said prayer is a train, and faith is the engine.[3] Prayer and faith. Faith and prayer. Prayer and faith. Prayer and faith belong together.

Let's look at Mark 9 to see how Jesus addressed the issue of prayer and faith:

> When they returned to the other disciples, they saw a large crowd surrounding them, and some teachers of religious law were arguing with them. When the crowd saw Jesus, they were overwhelmed with awe, and they ran to greet him.
>
> "What is all this arguing about?" Jesus asked.
>
> One of the men in the crowd spoke up and said, "Teacher, I brought my son so you could heal him. He is possessed by an evil spirit that won't let him talk. And whenever this spirit seizes him, it throws him violently to the ground. Then he foams at the mouth and grinds his teeth and becomes rigid. So I asked your disciples to cast out the evil spirit, but they couldn't do it."
>
> Jesus said to them, "You faithless people! How long must I be with you? How long must I put up with you? Bring the boy to me." So they brought the boy. But when the evil spirit saw Jesus, it threw the child into a violent convulsion, and he fell to the ground, writhing and foaming at the mouth. "How long has this been happening?" Jesus asked the boy's father.
>
> He replied, "Since he was a little boy. The spirit often throws him into the fire or into water, trying to kill him. Have mercy on us and help us, *if you can*."
>
> Verses 14–22, emphasis added

I love Jesus' response. He had been traveling throughout the towns and cities healing the sick, and some of the people still did not believe He was God in the flesh and could perform miracles. With regard to the man's "if" remark, it was as though Jesus said, "What do you mean *if*? Why would you say *if* when you are talking to the all-powerful God?" The Bible says the man instantly cried out, "I do believe, but help me overcome my unbelief!" (verse 24).

Can you relate to this story? Do you keep worrying whether or not God is going to show up in your situation? Are you worried that He is not going to make it in time? Do you find yourself doubting that He can fix such an impossible thing? Genuine faith never doubts God's ability to answer prayer. Remember, pray and ask for what you want, but do not doubt in your heart.

> **Do not pray only because someone told you to pray but because prayer is the native language of faith.**

Believe me, angels are waiting for you to pray about the thing God has spoken over your life. They are waiting to do the bidding of those who pray and believe. Some of these unemployed angels are something like those dudes who stand outside gas stations looking for work. Those angels have nothing to do because the saints will not pray. I want the number of unemployed angels assigned to us to go down, so I encourage people to pray more. Do not pray only because someone told you to pray but because prayer is the native language of faith.

Have you forgotten how good God is to you? Have you forgotten what He has promised us? If not, then run to God in prayer with an expectancy that only He can satisfy. Remember Jesus' words:

> "Ask and it will be given to you; seek and you will find; knock and the door will be opened to you. For everyone who asks

receives; the one who seeks finds; and to the one who knocks, the door will be opened. Which of you, if your son asks for bread, will give him a stone? Or if he asks for a fish, will give him a snake? If you, then, though you are evil, know how to give good gifts to your children, how much more will your Father in heaven give good gifts to those who ask him!"

Matthew 7:7–11 NKJV

A Faith That Forgives

Having faith in God is the key to unprecedented spiritual growth and intimacy. But nothing can hinder a vibrant prayer life like unforgiveness. If you are going to pray in faith and access the supernatural storehouses while holding a grudge, please know your prayers will be blocked. If you want to know why certain things are not happening when you pray, examine your heart for hatred or pride. Jesus said, "And whenever you stand praying, if you have anything against anyone, forgive him, that your Father in heaven may also forgive your trespasses" (Mark 11:25 NKJV).

Offense is another prayer-blocker. If you are offended or you have offended someone and you are aware of it, but refuse to do anything about it, your prayers will be blocked. It will not matter how much faith you have; if you hold on to an offense, you will not experience the realization of God's promises or the answers to your prayers.

We will talk more about unforgiveness in a later chapter, but the bottom line is this: All of us should be quick to forgive and not to hold on to offenses. Keep your heart clean, keep having faith in God and keep asking. God wants to answer your prayers.

PRAYER

"I do believe, but help me overcome my unbelief!" Lord, I pray those words straight from the Bible. Recognizing how crucial faith is to the effectiveness of my prayers, I reach out to You with a plea for more faith. Help me to grow up, even as You keep me childlike. Help me trust You in a naturally supernatural way. I am confident that I can ask for this because of what You did at the cross. Amen.

4

Ten Hindrances to Answered Prayer

> The effectual fervent prayer of a righteous man availeth much.
>
> James 5:16 KJV

The Bible makes it clear beyond the shadow of a doubt that the Father hears and answers the prayers of His children:

> I have written this to you who believe in the name of the Son of God, so that you may know you have eternal life. And we are confident that he hears us whenever we ask for anything that pleases him. And since we know he hears us

when we make our requests, we also know that he will give us what we ask for.

1 John 5:13–15

Therefore, if we are not seeing answers to our prayers, we need to figure out why.

Internal Hindrances to Answered Prayer

When I (Pastor William) was in school, I learned about "internal locus of control" and "external locus of control," which concern the extent to which people feel they have power over the events in their lives. A person with internal locus of control believes that he or she can influence events and their outcomes, while someone with external locus of control blames outside forces for everything.[1]

People may tell you that they believe external forces are the reason for unanswered prayer—that the devil is coming against them. But I have found that more of the reasons for unanswered prayer are internal than external. Or to put it a different way, perhaps you can effect internal changes that will allow your prayers to be answered.

In order to receive answers to prayer, you need to understand what is keeping you back. You cannot pray if you think you are just talking to the sky.

As we said previously, prayerlessness is one of the manifestations of unbelief. But another reason people sometimes stop praying is because they get frustrated with not seeing answers. In order to receive answers to prayer, you need to understand what is keeping you back. You cannot pray if you think you are just talking to the sky. Instead, you want to walk in power with the authority, maturity and joy of answered prayer.

Please embrace what we share in this chapter, because it can change your life, and it can certainly change your outcomes. Countless hindrances to prayer could be pointed out, but we are going to focus only on what we consider to be the ten most common ones.

1. Unconfessed Sin

Isaiah said, "Listen! The LORD's arm is not too weak to save you, nor is his ear too deaf to hear you call. It's your sins that have cut you off from God. Because of your sins, he has turned away and will not listen anymore" (Isaiah 59:1–2).

Sin separates us from God. We need to confess our sin to God and repent and stop fooling ourselves about it.

> If we claim we have no sin, we are only fooling ourselves and not living in the truth. But if we confess our sins to him, he is faithful and just to forgive us our sins and to cleanse us from all wickedness. If we claim we have not sinned, we are calling God a liar and showing that his word has no place in our hearts.
>
> 1 John 1:8–10

If you are living with unconfessed sin, make no mistake: It is blocking your prayers. In fact, for sure sin will be the primary hindrance to your prayers.

> Come and listen, all you who fear God, and I will tell you what he did for me. For I cried out to him for help, praising him as I spoke. *If I had not confessed the sin in my heart, the*

Lord would not have listened. But God did listen! He paid attention to my prayer. Praise God, who did not ignore my prayer or withdraw his unfailing love from me.

Psalm 66:16–20, emphasis added

The psalmist confessed his sin, and as a result God listened to his prayer. To underline its importance, let's now quote it from the Passion Translation (emphasis added):

All you lovers of God who want to please him, come and listen, and I'll tell you what he did for me. I cried aloud to him with all my heart and he answered me! Now my mouth overflows with the highest praise. Yet *if I had closed my eyes to my sin, the Lord God would have closed his ears to my prayer.* But praises rise to God, for he paid attention to my prayer and answered my cry to him! I will forever praise this God who didn't close his heart when I prayed and never said no when I asked him for help. He never once refused to show me his tender love.

Not confessing our sin to God hinders our prayers, but so does not confessing our sins to others. That part is harder for many people to hear. They feel that, as difficult as it may feel to confess their sins to God, at least it is silent and private, whereas speaking them out loud to someone else is too humiliating.

This does not square with what James (the brother of Jesus and the leader of the first "mother church" in Jerusalem) wrote to believers:

Are any of you suffering hardships? You should pray. Are any of you happy? You should sing praises. Are any of you sick? You should call for the elders of the church to come and pray over you, anointing you with oil in the name of the Lord. Such a prayer offered in faith will heal the sick, and the Lord will make you well. And if you have committed any sins, you will be forgiven. *Confess your sins to each other and pray for each other so that you may be healed.* The earnest prayer of a righteous person has great power and produces wonderful results.

James 5:13–16, emphasis added

The Message puts verses 16–18 this way:

> Make this your common practice: Confess your sins to each other and pray for each other so that you can live together whole and healed. The prayer of a person living right with God is something powerful to be reckoned with. Elijah, for instance, human just like us, prayed hard that it wouldn't rain, and it didn't—not a drop for three and a half years. Then he prayed that it would rain, and it did. The showers came and everything started growing again.

The people who prayed for these supernatural miracles were not superheroes. It was not Batman or Superman or Iron Man who performed these signs. A person just like you, who was in a righteous position with God, prayed earnestly, and God answered. The people in the Bible are not characters in a storybook. Moses, Elijah, Jeremiah and all of them were people just like you and me. God did not answer them because they were superhuman. He answered them because they were righteous and fervent in prayer. Part of becoming righteous involves confessing our sins to God and other people.

Because we do not usually like the idea of confessing our faults before others, we may not know what that looks like. Here is how one commentary explained it:

> Does this mean that believers are to go around confessing all their intimacies and ugliness? No! This is not what this passage is talking about. It is referring to certain types of sin or to certain times when we have to confess our sins. We should confess our sins . . .
> - when the sin has been a wrong or injustice done against someone else.
> - when we have misled or lied to someone.
> - when we have offended someone or caused someone to stumble and sin.
> - when restitution should be made.
> - when we publicly committed some crime and public forgiveness is required.[2]

Sometimes a trusted minister or Christian counselor may be able to help us in seeking restoration before God and man. Counseling is not bad. Some people go to the altar seeking prayer about things they need to talk to a counselor about. We tell them what the Bible says, and they may say that they have done that. But if they keep returning to the altar over and over for the same problem, it may be time to recommend a counselor.

Some people think that all problems are spiritual and that if someone is struggling with a habitual sin, a stronghold needs to be broken off their lives in prayer. But the fact is, there are no shortcuts. After the devil is cast out, the person may need to go talk to somebody to help them change their lives, lest the spirit come back. (If it does, Matthew 12:43–45 says it will return seven times worse.) They do not realize that the root problem is still there, and that prayers may be blocked because of that. Confessing to a counselor may bring full freedom.

2. Lack of Faith

Another reason your prayers may not be answered is a lack of faith. Remember, our faith must be placed in God. By itself, "faith" does not do anything. It is the God in whom you believe who does the work. Faith does not move mountains; God does. So we need to have faith *in* God.

James gives this advice:

> If any of you lacks wisdom, let him ask of God, who gives to all liberally and without reproach, and it will be given to him. But let him ask in faith, with no doubting, for he who doubts is like a wave of the sea driven and tossed by the wind. For let not that man suppose that he will receive anything from the Lord; he is a double-minded man, unstable in all his ways.
>
> James 1:5–8 NKJV

If you do not have faith in God, the answers to your prayers will be hindered. If you are doubting if God can do the thing you are asking Him to do, you are not going to see the answer. That is why the writer of Hebrews says, "It is impossible to please God without faith. Anyone who wants to come to him must believe that God exists and that he rewards those who sincerely seek him" (Hebrews 11:6).

Jesus said,

> "Have faith in God. For assuredly, I say to you, whoever says to this mountain, 'Be removed and be cast into the sea,' and

does not doubt in his heart, but believes that those things he says will be done, he will have whatever he says. Therefore I say to you, whatever things you ask when you pray, believe that you receive them, and you will have them."

Mark 11:22–24 NKJV

If you have faith in God—not in yourself or in your spouse or in your job, but in God—and you pray according to His will, you will receive answers to your prayers.

3. Self-Dependence

Another reason we fail to see answers to prayer is because we fail to ask God, thinking we can manage the situation ourselves. James makes it very clear:

You want what you don't have, so you scheme and kill to get it. You are jealous of what others have, but you can't get it, so you fight and wage war to take it away from them. Yet you don't have what you want because you don't ask God for it. And even when you ask, you don't get it because your motives are all wrong—you want only what will give you pleasure.

James 4:2–3

To see answers to prayer, you must learn to depend on God, not on yourself. Paul wrote, "How foolish can you be? After starting your new lives in the Spirit, why are you now trying to become perfect by your own human effort?" (Galatians 3:3). Prayer requires humility; we must fully surrender to God, and we must trust His will and His ways. And His ways are not our ways (see Isaiah 55:8). Whenever you are depending upon your own ability and trusting your own wisdom, you will not be praying as you ought, and you will not see answers to your prayers. That leads us into the next hindrance to answered prayer.

4. Wrong Motives

Again, as James 4:3 states, wrong motives prevent you from getting answers from God. When you are praying for what *you* want instead of what God wants, you will not see answers to your prayers because you are praying amiss. Perhaps you are praying for riches or comfort or success just because you want to feel secure and better than others. Perhaps you are praying for relief from some painful situation without regard to the fact that God may want to use that situation to bring someone (maybe even you) to Himself. Perhaps you are praying out loud largely so that you can impress the people who hear you.

Just be wary of presuming to think that you know better than God, because of course you do not!

Do a motive check whenever your prayers seem to be faltering. Ask the Holy Spirit to show you if something is wrong. Ask Him to teach you right motives (see John 14:26). He is the best Counselor in the universe.

5. Unforgiveness

Look again at Mark 11:24–25: "I tell you, you can pray for anything, and if you believe that you've received it, it will be yours. But when you are praying, first forgive anyone you are holding a grudge against, so that your Father in heaven will forgive your sins, too."

An unforgiving spirit is a prayer-blocker. That cannot be emphasized too much. If you want to see your prayers answered, let the Holy Spirit work on you. Ask Him to reveal anyone you need to forgive, and then forgive that person. Unforgiveness and offense are among the most common hindrances to answered prayer.

6. Offense

Being offended, or having unreconciled wrongs, always blocks prayers. Jesus said, "You have heard that our ancestors were told, 'You must not murder. If you commit murder, you are subject to judgment.' But I say, if you are even angry with someone, you are subject to judgment!" (Matthew 5:21–22). We fail to realize that being mad at others can actually block our prayers.

Jesus went on to say,

> "If you call someone an idiot, you are in danger of being brought before the court. And if you curse someone, you are in danger of the fires of hell. So if you are presenting a sacrifice at the altar in the Temple and you suddenly remember that someone has something against you, leave your sacrifice there at the altar. Go and be reconciled to that person. Then come and offer your sacrifice to God."
>
> Matthew 5:22–24

You cannot be at the altar with your hands lifted in worship when you are offended with someone, perhaps even someone in the same room. You may wish that somehow God would get that person, maybe strike him or her with lightning on the way to church. You hope the person will go to the second service so you do not have to cross paths in the first service. Guess what? Your being offended is not okay. Hanging on to your offense blocks your prayers and your blessing.

7. Pretentiousness

When you pray pretentiously, you are praying so that everybody will think you are spiritual, but God knows what is in your heart. You can fool the people around you, but you cannot fool God. Some people prefer to ignore this fact. They would rather keep up the charade so that others will think more highly of them instead of saying, "I need You, Jesus," and letting Him change their lives.

Praying to impress others, hoping everyone will think you are spiritual, will keep your prayers from being answered because you are not being honest before God. Jesus said,

> "And when you pray, you shall not be like the hypocrites. For they love to pray standing in the synagogues and on the corners of the streets, that they may be seen by men. Assuredly, I say to you, they have their reward. But you, when you pray, go into your room, and when you have shut your door, pray to your Father who is in the secret place; and your Father who sees in secret will reward you openly. And when you pray, do not use vain repetitions as the heathen do. For they think that they will be heard for their many words. Therefore do not be like them."
>
> Matthew 6:5–8 NKJV

When you pray, be honest. When you pray simply to make other people think you are spiritual, that will be your reward. But if you pray in private, honest before God, your prayers will not be hindered.

How weird it is to hear someone trying to sound deeply spiritual when they are not. They are just being pretentious—and ridiculous, like someone trying to swim in two inches of water, which is a complete waste of time. Be sincere before God so your prayers will not be hindered.

8. Idolatry

An idol is anything that has preeminence or top priority in our lives, anything that we give our love to. If you remember, idolatry was forbidden by God in the Ten Commandments:

> "You must not have any other god but me.
>
> "You must not make for yourself an idol of any kind or an image of anything in the heavens or on the earth or in the sea. You must not bow down to them or worship them, for I, the LORD your God, am a jealous God who will not tolerate your affection for any other gods. I lay the sins of the parents upon their children; the entire family is affected—even children in the third and fourth generations of those who reject me. But I lavish unfailing love for a thousand generations on those who love me and obey my commands."
>
> Exodus 20:3–6

This did not keep the people from worshiping idols, and God noticed, as Ezekiel prophesied:

> Some of the leaders of Israel approached me and sat down with me. GOD's Message came to me: "Son of Man, these people have installed idols in their hearts. They have embraced the wickedness that will ruin them. Why should I even bother with their prayers? Therefore tell them, 'The Message of GOD, the Master: All in Israel who install idols in

their hearts and embrace the wickedness that will ruin them and still have the gall to come to a prophet, be on notice: I, GOD, will step in and personally answer them as they come dragging along their mob of idols. I am ready to go to work on the hearts of the house of Israel, all of whom have left me for their idols.'"

Ezekiel 14:1–5 MSG

If you have not put God first and God is not answering your prayers, do not go to a prophet in an effort to get an answer that God wants to give you Himself! One of the reasons people may seek out a prophet for prayer is because something is blocking their own prayers, but God wants to answer them Himself. No prophet can give you what you are supposed to receive from God on your own.

One of the reasons some prophetic churches seem to lack balance is because churches that raise up prophets also sometimes inadvertently raise up a congregation who are too lazy to hear God for themselves. They have a bunch of weak-kneed believers who refuse to pray, hoping that one day if they sit the right way, wear the right thing or give the right amount, God will give the prophet a word for them. They want to hear from a person instead of hearing from God. God may not want to speak to any of them through a prophet, because He can speak to everyone directly.

God wants to answer your prayer, and He wants to speak to you. Receiving a personal word from another person is not the same as receiving a word straight from God Himself. Yes, God loves you enough to give you direction through a man or woman when you find yourself directionless and drifting, but that is not His preferred method of talking to you. His preferred method of talking to you is through His Word and through answered prayer.

Do not allow a prophetic atmosphere to make you a lazy intercessor. Make God preeminent and tear down your idols (meaning everything that you put first), and He will answer you. Prophets communicate the plans of God and His heart and mind, but their words are not supposed to be substitutes for having a personal relationship with God and hearing from Him yourself.

9. Indifference to God's Word

Being indifferent to God's Word blocks you from receiving answers: "God detests the prayers of a person who ignores the law" (Proverbs 28:9). And if God is speaking to you through His Word and you ignore it, do not bother to go to the altar asking for prayer.

Here is the same verse in *The Message*: "God has no use for the prayers of the people who won't listen to him." Can it get any plainer than that? The admonition is clear even in the older English of the King James Version: "He that turneth away his ear from hearing the law, even his prayer shall be abomination."

10. Domestic Disturbances

Not every hindrance to prayer is entirely internal and personal; some involve our reactions to ongoing circumstances. For instance, domestic breakdowns and disturbances at home will definitely hinder your prayers.

Many women in the church say, "My husband does not believe. What should I do? Should I leave him?" No. Live a godly life, and that will speak to him. Many of the women in our church have come to us after a while, saying, "Here is my husband. He is now attending church." They have followed Peter's advice: "You wives must accept the authority of your husbands. Then, even if some refuse to obey the Good News, your godly lives will speak to them without any words. They will be won over" (1 Peter 3:1).

On the flip side, a wife is not always the Christian spouse. Once a husband came and said he felt that Deeper Fellowship was his home church, but his wife would not attend. I told him not to come to church without her. He got really quiet. When one Sunday I saw him, I asked him, "Where's your wife?"

He said, "She didn't come."

And I said, "Then go home."

I was not trying to be mean or insensitive. I wanted him to see the importance of being reconciled and one in thought with his wife. Husbands must give honor to their wives, submitting to one another, not domineering over them. A man cannot command his wife as if she is his pet, because she is his equal in the Christian faith.

Some couples decide to go to different churches, but the Bible does not support that idea.

Peter advised couples as follows:

They [unbelieving husbands] will be won over by observing your pure and reverent lives. Don't be concerned about the outward beauty of fancy hairstyles, expensive jewelry, or beautiful clothes. You should clothe yourselves instead with the beauty that comes from within, the unfading beauty of a gentle and quiet spirit, which is so precious to God. This is how the holy women of old made themselves beautiful. They put their trust in God and accepted the authority of their husbands. For instance, Sarah obeyed her husband, Abraham, and called him her master. You are her daughters when you do what is right without fear of what your husbands might do.

In the same way, you husbands must give honor to your wives. Treat your wife with understanding as you live together. She may be weaker than you are, but she is your equal partner in God's gift of new life. Treat her as you should so your prayers will not be hindered.

1 Peter 3:1–7

Are you having discord in your marriage? Are you not talking to each other? That hinders your prayers.

A friend and I were talking one day, and he mentioned that he and his wife had gotten into an argument and now they were not really talking to each other. As the conversation went on, I shared a need that I had. My friend said, "Oh man, well, let me pray for you!"

I said, "Don't bother"—true story—"because your prayers are hindered right now."

I explained why I had said that, and a couple of hours later, he called me and said, "I can pray for you now."

Not talking to your spouse, being selfish and failing to deny yourself, not being supportive, having sex with anyone other than your spouse—all of those things will hinder your prayers. If you are cheating on your spouse, the only prayer God is going to hear is a prayer of repentance!

We do not like to talk about this stuff. We want to act as if it does not happen in the Church. But denying that these things happen will not change the reality; they may be why God is not answering your prayers.

Another domestic issue that can hinder your prayers is never being home. If you are always out, hanging out with friends or even working, and you are coming home at all sorts of hours, that can hinder your prayers. When your life is out of balance because you are too busy playing video games or golfing or shopping, just know that if you are not seeing answers to your prayers, you need to go home. You need to reprioritize your time.

Do Not Blame the Devil

We just looked at ten reasons our prayers can be hindered, and nine of them are completely internal. Many people think their prayers are not being answered because of external, satanic resistance. They rarely consider any other possibility. The devil has a lot of people fooled, thinking he is the cause of their problems when in reality, the hindrances are internal. They give the devil too much credit. They blame the devil for their prayers not being answered while they are holding

> **You need to understand: The devil cannot stop the answers to your prayers, but you can.**

on to offense or unforgiveness. They blame the devil when the problem is the discord they have allowed to fester in their homes.

You need to understand: The devil cannot stop the answers to your prayers, but you can. The only thing the devil can do is to slow down the manifestation of the answer. Only you can stop an answer from coming.

To unlock prayer in your life, make sure everything is unblocked.

If you are not seeing answered prayer, ask God to take away everything in your life that might be hindering the answer from coming.

The enemy can delay the answers, but he cannot actually block them, as we learn in the account of Daniel and the prince [evil spirit] of Persia in Daniel 10:12–14. God's answer to Daniel's prayer was on the way from the moment he uttered it. The evil principality who controlled Persia made a concerted effort to slow down the answer. In the end, Daniel's powerful prayer would be answered perfectly, but he remained in the dark about the results for a period of time.

If you are living a life that is righteous before God and your prayers seem to be blocked, just stay in a righteous position, avoiding the ten prayer-blockers we talked about, and do not move. You might not see the answer today or tomorrow or the next day, but you can be sure of this: If God spoke to you and promised it to you, and if you prayed about it, it is coming.

And while you are waiting for the answer to come, give God praise for it. Start giving Him thanks in advance for it. You may not know when it is coming, but decide today that you will not move until you see it.

PRAYER

Dear God, You are supreme in every way and yet You pay attention to my most feeble prayer. Keep me mindful of what You have taught me in Your Word, so that my prayers can flow unimpeded to Your throne. I do not want to keep blaming the devil when my prayers seem to bounce down off the ceiling. Instead, show me how to repent of my sin and lack of faith. Convict me of depending too much on my own strength and resources. Keep me from becoming indifferent to Your Word, which is life to me. According to Your great mercy and unfailing love, support me in all of my failings and lead me past all hindrances. I trust You alone because of Jesus. Amen.

5

Ten Benefits of Prayer

Pray without ceasing.

1 Thessalonians 5:17 NKJV

These are the words of the apostle Paul. Reading the verse in several versions serves to lay emphasis on his command: In the New Living Translation, we are told to "never stop praying." The Christian Standard Bible puts it this way: "pray constantly." The Good News Translation says, "Pray at all times." *The Message* tells us to "pray all the time."

No matter what translation you use, the message is clear: Pray, pray and pray some more!

Prayer is not just something we do for ten minutes in the morning and another ten minutes at night. We are told to pray all the time. Why is this? Because we receive certain benefits as a result of our prayer. Certain things happen when we pray that will not happen when we do not. In this chapter, we will look at ten of those benefits so you can see what is at your disposal when you awaken to the power of prayer.

1. Peace

There is an answer to worry and anxiety, and it is a supernatural one. The peace of God is the complete answer to worry and anxiety, and you obtain it through prayer:

> Don't worry about anything; instead, pray about everything. Tell God what you need, and thank him for all he has done. Then you will experience God's peace, which exceeds anything we can understand. His peace will guard your hearts and minds as you live in Christ Jesus.
>
> Philippians 4:6–7

When you pray, you receive peace. This is what Jesus told us:

> "That is why I tell you not to worry about everyday life— whether you have enough food and drink, or enough clothes to wear. Isn't life more than food, and your body more than clothing? Look at the birds. They don't plant or harvest or store food in barns, for your heavenly Father feeds them. And aren't you far more valuable to him than they are? Can all your worries add a single moment to your life?
>
> "And why worry about your clothing? Look at the lilies of the field and how they grow. They don't work or make their clothing, yet Solomon in all his glory was not dressed as beautifully as they are. And if God cares so wonderfully for wildflowers that are here today and thrown into the fire

tomorrow, he will certainly care for you. Why do you have so little faith?

"So don't worry about these things, saying, "What will we eat? What will we drink? What will we wear?" These things dominate the thoughts of unbelievers, but your heavenly Father already knows all your needs. Seek the Kingdom of God above all else, and live righteously, and he will give you everything you need.

"So don't worry about tomorrow, for tomorrow will bring its own worries. Today's trouble is enough for today."

Matthew 6:25–34

Worry is for nonbelievers. Prayer and peace are for believers. This is because genuine prayer and worry can never coexist.

Why is this? Because we are not praying to ourselves. Praying and worrying at the same time means that you consider your own power equal to God's, or at least that you believe your ability to effect change is equal to or greater than God's ability to effect change. If you are praying and you are also tossing and turning in your bed, then you have not given the issue to Him yet. Your tossing and turning shows you do not believe He is God. (Instead, subconsciously, you think *you* are.)

Genuine prayer and worry can never coexist.

Tell yourself, *Don't worry about it. Pray about it.* For real, though. That is not just a cliché. Don't worry about it. Pray about it.

Obey what the Bible says: "Give all your worries and cares to God, for he cares about you" (1 Peter 5:7). It does not say "Give all your worries and your cares to your best friend," or "Give all your worries and cares to your spouse." If you are married, there are some things you need to talk about, and there are other things you need to pray about. Get God's wisdom. Get God's counsel. Get God's peace. Stop saddling your spouse with things that you should be giving to God.

Learn how to give your cares and worries to God and leave them there! If you go forward at church and lay a burden down at the altar, you do not pick it back up when you return to your seat. You leave it there. In the same way, when you give your worries to God in prayer, leave them with Him. When you do, you will receive the peace of God.

2. Revelation, Discernment and Direction

Revelation, discernment and direction (instruction and guidance) will come to you when you pray, especially if you ask God for them. In the presence of God, something just opens up in your spirit and mind, and you will find that you are not only more receptive to His input, but that you also receive insights regularly. This is certainly a major benefit of prayer.

Revelation: Prayer leads to revelation. The Bible makes this clear:

> While Jeremiah was still confined in the courtyard of the guard, the LORD gave him this second message: "This is what the LORD says—the LORD who made the earth, who formed and established it, whose name is the LORD: Ask me and I will tell you remarkable secrets you do not know about things to come."
>
> Jeremiah 33:1–3

Have you ever wondered why certain people get such deep levels of revelation on a regular basis? It is because of their prayer life. We all read the same Bible, but not all of us are walking in the same level of revelation. The reason for that is because not all of us are committed to prayer in the same degree. If you are believing for something to be revealed by God, that will not happen without prayer because prayer leads to revelation.

In other words, revelation is not automatic; it is a result of prayer.

This passage from Joshua 9 is long, but it will help you to understand this concept:

> But when the people of Gibeon heard what Joshua had done to Jericho and Ai, they resorted to deception to save themselves. They sent ambassadors to Joshua, loading their donkeys with weathered saddlebags and old, patched wineskins. They put on worn-out, patched sandals and ragged clothes. And the bread they took with them was dry and moldy. When they arrived at the camp of Israel at Gilgal, they told Joshua and the men of Israel, "We have come from a distant land to ask you to make a peace treaty with us."
>
> The Israelites replied to these Hivites, "How do we know you do not live nearby? For if you do, we cannot make a treaty with you."
>
> They replied, "We are your servants."
>
> "But who are you?" Joshua demanded. "Where do you come from?"
>
> They answered, "Your servants have come from a very distant country. We have heard of the might of the LORD your God and of all he did in Egypt. We have also heard what he did to the two Amorite kings east of the Jordan River—King

Sihon of Heshbon and King Og of Bashan (who lived in Ashtaroth). So our elders and all our people instructed us, 'Take supplies for a long journey. Go meet with the people of Israel and tell them, "We are your servants; please make a treaty with us."'

"This bread was hot from the ovens when we left our homes. But now, as you can see, it is dry and moldy. These wineskins were new when we filled them, but now they are old and split open. And our clothing and sandals are worn out from our very long journey."

So the Israelites examined their food, but they did not consult the LORD. Then Joshua made a peace treaty with them and guaranteed their safety, and the leaders of the community ratified their agreement with a binding oath.

Three days after making the treaty, they learned that these people actually lived nearby!

Joshua 9:3–16

When the people of Gibeon heard that God had given victory to the Israelites at Jericho and Ai, they knew it would be crazy to fight them, so they planned to deceive them instead. They sent ambassadors to Joshua, making it look as though they had been traveling for a long time. They lied to him, saying, "We have come from a distant land to ask you to make a peace treaty with us."

You see, the Israelites had committed themselves not to making treaties with anyone who lived nearby. That is why the Gibeonites made up their story about how far they had traveled to meet with Joshua. Their tale was nothing but a bunch of lies.

The Israelites examined their moldy food, but they didn't

pray. Joshua made the peace treaty with them, only to find out three days later that they actually lived nearby. If the Israelites had prayed, the Lord could have revealed to them the truth of the situation.

Discernment: Because the Israelites did not pray and consult the Lord and instead used natural means to make their decision, they missed out on a key benefit of prayer—discernment. When you pray, you receive discernment.

Just because something is good does not verify that it is from God. That is why we should not make decisions without praying. And certainly just because something looks like the easiest path does not mean it is God. Sometimes God will take you on a journey that you would prefer not to go on. But God knows exactly why He is sending you in that direction. He knows what He is protecting you from.

You can probably think of some decisions you made and then regretted shortly afterward. Yet I doubt you will ever regret a decision as much as the Israelites regretted theirs. By the time the Israelites had discovered the truth and realized that they were supposed to have destroyed the Gibeonites, it was too late. Their misapprehension and resulting decision affected the welfare of their entire nation for a very long time, because now they had bound themselves with an oath before God that they would never destroy these people. The Israelites ended up in a real mess—all because they did not pray before making their decision.

Direction: If you pray, God will give you direction. A story from the life of David illustrates this prayer benefit.

Three days later, when David and his men arrived home at their town of Ziklag, they found that the Amalekites had made a raid into the Negev and Ziklag; they had crushed Ziklag and burned it to the ground. They had carried off the women and children and everyone else but without killing anyone.

When David and his men saw the ruins and realized what had happened to their families, they wept until they could weep no more. David's two wives, Ahinoam from Jezreel and Abigail, the widow of Nabal from Carmel, were among those captured. David was now in great danger because all his men were very bitter about losing their sons and daughters, and they began to talk of stoning him. But David found strength in the LORD his God.

Then he said to Abiathar the priest, "Bring me the ephod!" So Abiathar brought it. Then David asked the LORD, "Should I chase after this band of raiders? Will I catch them?"

And the LORD told him, "Yes, go after them. You will surely recover everything that was taken from you!"

1 Samuel 30:1–8

David went into the presence of God asking for direction, and when he prayed, God spoke to him. The account does not read "God showed him," but rather "He told him." This is important to grasp, because too many people start moving before they hear from God, and they end up going their own way.

3. Boldness

Another benefit of prayer is that prayer releases boldness. A passage from the book of Acts shows us this:

While Peter and John were speaking to the people, they were confronted by the priests, the captain of the Temple guard, and some of the Sadducees. These leaders were very disturbed that Peter and John were teaching the people that through Jesus there is a resurrection of the dead. They arrested them and, since it was already evening, put them in jail until morning. But many of the people who heard their message believed it, so the number of men who believed now totaled about 5,000.

The next day the council of all the rulers and elders and teachers of religious law met in Jerusalem. Annas the high priest was there, along with Caiaphas, John, Alexander, and other relatives of the high priest. They brought in the two disciples and demanded, "By what power, or in whose name, have you done this?"

Then Peter, filled with the Holy Spirit, said to them, "Rulers and elders of our people, are we being questioned today because we've done a good deed for a crippled man? Do you want to know how he was healed? Let me clearly state to all of you and to all the people of Israel that he was healed by the powerful name of Jesus Christ the Nazarene, the man you crucified but whom God raised from the dead. For Jesus is the one referred to in the Scriptures, where it says, 'The stone that you builders rejected has now become the cornerstone.' There is salvation in no one else! God has given no other name under heaven by which we must be saved."

The members of the council were amazed when they saw the boldness of Peter and John, for they could see that they were ordinary men with no special training in the Scriptures. They also recognized them as men who had been with Jesus. But since they could see the man who had been healed standing right there among them, there was nothing the council could say.

Acts 4:1–14

Let me emphasize that "the members of the council were amazed when they saw the *boldness* of Peter and John, for they could see they were ordinary men. *They also recognized them as men who had been with Jesus.*" Every time I read that, I just love it. You cannot refute fruit.

The members of the council did not know what to do with Peter and John. They could not deny that they had performed a miracle, but they wanted to keep them from evangelizing any further. So they commanded them to never again speak or teach in Jesus' name. But Peter and John replied, "Do you think God wants us to obey you rather than him?" (Acts 4:19). That was boldness!

The council threatened Peter and John further, but they finally let them go because they did not know how to punish the men without starting a riot. Everyone was praising God for the miraculous sign He had done when He healed the man who had been lame for more than forty years. As soon as Peter and John were freed, they returned to the other believers and told them what had been said.

The Bible goes on to say that "when they heard the report, all the believers lifted their voices together in prayer to God" (Acts 4:24). Their prayer resulted in more boldness: "The meeting place shook, and they were all filled with the Holy Spirit. Then they preached the word of God with boldness" (Acts 4:31).

One of the benefits of prayer is boldness. Begin to pray, and you can walk in boldness instead of being timid or afraid. You can walk in boldness because you are serving a God who not only hears, but answers unfailingly. And there is no problem too big for Him.

In addition, just as prayer produces boldness, a lifestyle

of boldness causes others to ask God for boldness. That is what happened in Acts 4. When Peter and John told the church how bold they had been when they stood before the council, the church said, "We want that, too." They lifted their voices and prayed, "And now, O Lord, hear their threats, and give us, your servants, great boldness in preaching your word" (Acts 4:29). When they prayed for it, God gave them the boldness they had asked for.

4. Answers

Other religions pray to gods who do not talk. Our God is not mute, nor is He deaf. Why would we sing to Him if He could not hear? Why would we pray to Him if we He could not hear us? He hears and He answers. The fourth (and obvious) benefit of prayer is that it gets results—answers. Jesus said:

> "Keep on asking, and you will receive what you ask for. Keep on seeking, and you will find. Keep on knocking, and the door will be opened to you. For everyone who asks, receives. Everyone who seeks, finds. And to everyone who knocks, the door will be opened."
>
> Matthew 7:7–8

5. Confirmation of Your Identity

Jesus goes on to say,

> "You parents—if your children ask for a loaf of bread, do you give them a stone instead? Or if they ask for a fish, do you give them a snake? Of course not! So if you sinful people

know how to give good gifts to your children, how much more will your heavenly Father give good gifts to those who ask him."

Matthew 7: 9–11

The fifth benefit of prayer is confirmation of who we are as the children of God. We are not just praying to a distant God. We are praying to our Father. When Jesus said to pray, "Our Father . . . " (Matthew 6:9), He was confirming our identity as sons and daughters of God. You cannot be a son or daughter without a father.

Even if you had an absent father or a traumatic upbringing or you did not feel supported as a child, every time you pray you are reconfirming your identity as a son or a daughter of a loving Father. Your earthly father may have walked out on you, but your God will not. Your heavenly Father has always been there, and He will always be there for you, because you belong to Him.

6. Access to the Supernatural

It should go without saying that prayer gives you access to the supernatural realm.

The prayer of faith brings you directly into the presence of God. You do not have to be extraordinary to pray the prayer of faith. James wrote about the prayer of faith, and he cited Elijah's prayer as an example, noting that Elijah was an ordinary man just like us, but when he prayed that it would not rain, the heavens were shut (see James 5:17). This miracle did not happen because Elijah was a prophet. It happened because Elijah prayed in faith.

James had just recommended prayer as the way to obtain the blessings of heaven:

> Are any of you suffering hardships? You should pray. Are any of you happy? You should sing praises. Are any of you sick? You should call for the elders of the church to come and pray over you, anointing you with oil in the name of the Lord. Such a prayer offered in faith will heal the sick, and the Lord will make you well. And if you have committed any sins, you will be forgiven.
>
> James 5:13–15

Please do not think that your pastor's prayers count more in heaven than yours do. The fact is that when anyone prays in faith, he or she will see results. When you pray, you will see a supernatural manifestation of the Spirit of God; access to the supernatural is a key benefit of prayer. It is not a benefit only to prophets or pastors or worship leaders—this benefit belongs to any child of God who prays in faith.

Do not think that your pastor's prayers count more in heaven than yours do. The fact is that when anyone prays in faith, he or she will see results.

As Bible teacher Sinclair Ferguson put it, the prayer of faith is "believing God's revealed Word, taking hold of His covenant commitment to it, and asking Him to keep it."[1] In other words, the prayer of faith asks God to accomplish what He has already promised. In Elijah's case, he declared, "God, look at the conditions on the ground here. You said [in Deuteronomy 28:15–24] that if the people behaved like this, You would shut up the heavens. So now I am asking You to do what You said."

That is the prayer of faith: "Father, do what You said You'd do." Do not think you just need to believe harder, because that is not the key. Attach your faith to the Word of God, and when you ask God to do what is in His Word, you are praying the prayer of faith.

When Elijah prayed for there to be no rain, he was laying hold of what God had promised. Base your prayers on what God has said in His Word. When someone is sick, remind the Lord of His Word: "By His stripes we are healed" (Isaiah 53:5 NKJV).

The prayer of faith gives you access to the supernatural realm of God. Joshua's prayer illustrates this in an exceptional way:

> On the day the LORD gave the Israelites victory over the Amorites, Joshua prayed to the LORD in front of all the people of Israel. He said, "Let the sun stand still over Gibeon, and the moon over the valley of Aijalon." So the sun stood still and the moon stayed in place until the nation of Israel had defeated its enemies. . . . The sun stayed in the middle of the sky, and it did not set as on a normal day. There has never been a day like this one before or since, when the LORD answered such a prayer. Surely the LORD fought for Israel that day!
>
> Joshua 10:12–14

When Joshua asked for the sun to stand still, he was praying the prayer of faith, because he had a promise of victory from God (see Joshua 10:8). His prayer opened up supernatural timelessness and prolonged the daylight until the enemy army could be vanquished.

Standing in the promises of God not only makes you able to pray boldly, but it also gives you access to God's supernatural power. You do not have to understand how God is going to answer your prayer; He will do whatever is necessary to fulfill His promise. You do not have to understand how it works. Joshua did not know what it would take for God to make the sun stand still, but he did not have to know. All he had to do was believe. (Joshua asked for the sun to stand still. Today, through modern science, we know that the miracle could not have been accomplished that way. The way God answered Joshua's prayer was by making the earth stop revolving around the sun, which is no less a miracle and which had the perfect results.) Our elementary minds may not understand the intricacies of what it takes to answer our prayers, but that does not stop our omnipotent God.

You do not need to understand the answer, you only have to believe for it. You do not have to have the "right words." You only have to pray what God has promised you boldly.

When a man or a woman asks you to pray for his or her healing, you may never understand how every muscle and tissue in that person's body works, but when you say, "In Jesus' name, be healed," the sick structures will start changing. Your prayer gives you access to the supernatural power of God. He hears and He answers.

7. Rejuvenation and Refreshment

Prayer rejuvenates, refreshes and replenishes you in every way. Even Jesus needed it: "Jesus often withdrew to the wilderness for prayer" (Luke 5:16). He needed that time to get recharged after pouring Himself out to so many people.

You can expect to have your strength replenished by God after He uses you. Always go to Him to get refilled after His Spirit has been poured out through you. Otherwise, you may think you accomplished everything yourself. Rejuvenation, refreshment and replenishment come from praying. That is why we pray not only before we minister but also after.

Jesus Himself often withdrew from the crowds of people. By seeking prayerful solitude, He was showing us that He could not minister to the world unless He also took time to be rejuvenated, refreshed and replenished by spending time with His Father. If Jesus, in whom the Spirit dwelled without limit, had to go away to pray, do we not need to do the same?

Many of us think rejuvenation comes through relaxation, but that benefits only your body. Your spirit needs to be refreshed, as well, and that happens through prayer.

Bodily refreshment comes through rest. Spiritual refreshment comes through prayer.

That may seem counterintuitive for those who view prayer only as an exertion because they forget that prayer is a refreshing dialogue. In prayer, not only do you talk to God, but He also talks to you. Not only do you minister to God, but He also ministers to you. This is why solitude is so often associated with prayer. In solitude, we quiet ourselves in God's presence.

Instead of crawling into His lap and rattling off our list of requests as if He were Santa Claus, we practice being silent in His presence first. Too often people who are learning the mechanics of prayer are not taught the value of silence. They fill up the silence with their requests and then leave without hearing from Him. But throughout Scripture, we discover that He is a God who talks. And many times, particularly with the Old Testament prophets, He would talk first, and then they would talk, not the other way around. The dialogue brings refreshment.

8. Wisdom

If you pray and ask for wisdom, you will receive it. James advises,

> Dear brothers and sisters, when troubles of any kind come your way, consider it an opportunity for great joy. For you know that when your faith is tested, your endurance has a chance to grow. So let it grow, for when your endurance is fully developed, you will be perfect and complete, needing nothing. If you need wisdom, ask our generous God, and he will give it to you. He will not rebuke you for asking.
>
> James 1:2–5

If you need wisdom for leadership, ask God. If you need wisdom to understand the season you are in, ask God. This is one of the benefits of prayer. Follow the example of Solomon, who pleased God by asking for wisdom:

> Solomon loved the LORD and followed all the decrees of his father, David. . . . The LORD appeared to Solomon in a dream, and God said, "What do you want? Ask, and I will give it to you!"
>
> Solomon replied, . . . "O LORD my God, you have made me king instead of my father, David, but I am like a little child who doesn't know his way around. And here I am in the midst of your own chosen people, a nation so great and numerous they cannot be counted! Give me an understanding

heart so that I can govern your people well and know the difference between right and wrong. For who by himself is able to govern this great people of yours?"

The Lord was pleased that Solomon had asked for wisdom. So God replied, "Because you have asked for wisdom in governing my people with justice and have not asked for a long life or wealth or the death of your enemies—I will give you what you asked for! I will give you a wise and understanding heart such as no one else has had or ever will have! And I will also give you what you did not ask for—riches and fame! No other king in all the world will be compared to you for the rest of your life! And if you follow me and obey my decrees and my commands as your father, David, did, I will give you a long life."

1 Kings 3:3, 5–14

When you pray, you receive wisdom from God. He will not rebuke you for asking, and it pleases Him that you do.

9. A New Perspective

Prayer changes your perspective. This is an important benefit, because the way you initially see things is not always correct. You will not know whether you are seeing something correctly until you pray.

Have you ever looked at your circumstances and thought, *Wait a minute, God. I am serving You. I am tithing. I am giving. I am praying. I am fasting. And I still can't make ends meet. Meanwhile, I see other people who curse You, and they have whatever they want. Come on, where's the justice?* That is how Asaph felt when he composed Psalm 73:

Truly God is good to Israel, to those whose hearts are pure. But as for me, I almost lost my footing. My feet were slipping, and I was almost gone. For I envied the proud when I saw them prosper despite their wickedness. They seem to live such painless lives; their bodies are so healthy and strong. They don't have troubles like other people; they're not plagued with problems like everyone else. . . . "What does God know?" they ask. "Does the Most High even know what's happening?"

Did I keep my heart pure for nothing? Did I keep myself innocent for no reason? I get nothing but trouble all day long; every morning brings me pain.

Psalm 73:1–5, 11, 13–14

Now, notice what happens when he spends time with God: "Then I went into your sanctuary, O God, and I finally understood the destiny of the wicked. Truly, you put them on a slippery path and send them sliding over the cliff to destruction" (verses 17–18).

After Asaph prayed, his perspective changed. He realized that gaining things in this world is not the goal. Some of us today need to get that revelation. We, particularly the Church in the Western world, can become so intoxicated by our wealth that all we want to do is be wealthy, but we have to remember that this life is temporary.

Asaph's perspective changed not only about the condition of others, but also about himself. He expresses himself in verses 21–22: "Then I realized that my heart was bitter, and I was all torn up inside. I was so foolish and ignorant—I must have seemed like a senseless animal to you."

Prayer not only gives you a different perspective about what you are seeing; it gives you a different perspective about yourself. In fact, if something about your heart does not get exposed while you are in the presence of God, you are not really praying. You are just talking to the ceiling.

Asaph did not only gain God's perspective about the people in the world and the condition of his own heart; he also recalled his place with God:

> Yet I still belong to you; you hold my right hand. You guide me with your counsel, leading me to a glorious destiny. Whom have I in heaven but you? I desire you more than anything on earth. My health may fail, and my spirit may grow weak, but God remains the strength of my heart; he is mine forever.
>
> Verses 23–26

All through prayer, Asaph acquired a right perspective about the world, himself and God. Prayer changes your perspective.

10. Forgiveness and Mercy

Confession is a form of prayer. You may not know what else to say, but you can always say, "God, I confess that I need You. I have not been living the way You want me to. Make me clean." We do not define sin; God, who is perfect and holy, determines what sin is. Laws on the earth will change, and what used to be wrong will be considered right based on the ruling of a judge, but the ultimate Judge never changes His mind.

Sin is anything that falls short of His perfect, holy standard. The bar is high—too high for us to reach without

Him. We get the help we need if we confess our sins, because He is faithful and just to forgive us and cleanse us from all wickedness (see 1 John 1:9). This is another major benefit of prayer—forgiveness and mercy.

God is so moved by a prayer for forgiveness that He allows believers to repent on behalf of nations. In this way, we extend the benefits of prayer. But only if we confess. Where does confession happen? In prayer.

We look forward to the Lord's return, as the Bible says we should. But when Jesus comes again, He will return as a judge. So while you are at the altar saying, "Even so, come, Lord Jesus," are you sure that everyone you know is going to be on the right side of judgment? If there is anybody in your life who is not saved, you should be praying for mercy.

Sometimes it may seem that the Lord is overly patient, giving unrepentant sinners second and third and fourth chances to turn to Him. But who are we to decide who should be saved, and when? The Lord is not being slow in returning; He is being patient. He is delaying His coming so people can be saved. Remember what Peter wrote: "The Lord isn't really being slow about his promise, as some people think. No, he is being patient for your sake. He does not want anyone to be destroyed, but wants everyone to repent" (2 Peter 3:9). The rest of what Peter wrote is important as well:

> Most importantly, I want to remind you that in the last days scoffers will come, mocking the truth and following their own desires. They will say, "What happened to the promise that Jesus is coming again? From before the times of our ancestors, everything has remained the same since the world was first created."

They deliberately forget that God made the heavens long ago by the word of His command, and he brought the earth out from the water and surrounded it with water. Then he used the water to destroy the ancient world with a mighty flood. And by the same word, the present heavens and earth have been stored up for fire. They are being kept for the day of judgment, when ungodly people will be destroyed.

But you must not forget this one thing, dear friends: A day is like a thousand years to the Lord, and a thousand years is like a day. *The Lord isn't really being slow about his promise, as some people think. No, he is being patient for your sake. He does not want anyone to be destroyed, but wants everyone to repent.* But the day of the Lord will come as unexpectedly as a thief. Then the heavens will pass away with a terrible noise, and the very elements themselves will disappear in fire, and the earth and everything on it will be found to deserve judgment.

2 Peter 3:3–10, emphasis added

The Lord is not being slow in coming again—nor is He being slow in answering your prayers. Rather, He is being supremely patient, delaying His coming so that more people can be saved.

Prayer for mercy is both individual and corporate. God looks for people who will enact the benefit of forgiveness for their cities, for their families and for their nations. He is looking for people who will say, "Have mercy on us, Lord. Pour out Your Spirit so that more people can come to know You. We know You are withholding Your coming because of Your love, because You want everybody to repent."

Have you ever prayed that God would be merciful to someone who does not know Him? I have been praying for one friend for twenty years. While everyone else is saying, "Lord Jesus, come anytime You want," I'm saying, "Not until this guy is saved," because I love him that much.

Prayer changes things. It changes us. It changes circumstances. It changes our perspective. Prayer gives us peace and boldness. But one of the most important benefits of prayer is that it gives us a voice in the heavenly council. That is what we will begin to explore together in the next chapter.

PRAYER

Father God, I want my praying to be as frequent and as natural as conversation, and I do not want to forget to pray. I want to taste and see that You are good, and that praying to You—besides bringing answers—has multiple benefits, too many to count. I pray that I will appreciate those benefits more every year, and that spending so much time in Your presence will change my character into Your likeness. Thank You for making prayer possible, and for always answering. In Jesus' name I pray, Amen.

6

The Divine Council

God has taken his place in the divine council; in the
midst of the gods he holds judgment.

Psalm 82:1 ESV

God never intended to have divine orchestration without
human participation. What do we mean by "divine orchestration"? We mean the magnificent way God works everything together for His perfect purposes, combining everything from crashing, crushing events to the tiniest whisper.
And how do we participate in His divine orchestration? Only
through prayer.

Prayer is a completely supernatural transaction. It takes
place in the spirit, and it affects things in the natural. Prayer
is the access point or the portal by which the realities of the

invisible world (the Kingdom of God) enter into the visible world (the earth).

In heaven, there is a divine council where spiritual transactions take place. The New Living Translation of Psalm 82:1 reads: "God presides over heaven's court; he pronounces judgment on the heavenly beings."

In this divine council or court, you and I have a seat because of what Jesus did on the cross. Our place on the divine council is so important that we are going to examine this subject over the next several chapters.

Seated in Heavenly Places

I want us to begin by looking at Ephesians 1:19–23, in which Paul tells us that Christ sits in the heavenly realms:

> I also pray that you will understand the incredible greatness of God's power for us who believe him. This is the same mighty power that raised Christ from the dead and seated him in the place of honor at God's right hand in the heavenly realms. Now he is far above any ruler or authority or power or leader or anything else—not only in this world but also in the world to come. God has put all things under the authority of Christ and has made him head over all things for the benefit of the church. And the church is his body; it is made full and complete by Christ, who fills all things everywhere with himself.
>
> Ephesians 1:19–23

God has put all things under the authority of Christ, who is seated at the right hand of God, and has made Him the head over all things for the benefit of the Church. The Church is His Body. It is made full and complete by Christ, who fills all things everywhere with Himself.

We see the same thing in the next chapter of the letter to the Ephesian church:

> But God is so rich in mercy, and he loved us so much, that even though we were dead because of our sins, he gave us life when he raised Christ from the dead. (It is only by God's grace that you have been saved!) For he raised us from the dead along with Christ and seated us with him in the heavenly realms because we are united with Christ Jesus.
>
> Ephesians 2:4–6

Verse 6 tells us Christ is seated in the heavenly places, and we are right there with Him. But how does that work? Colossians 3:1–3 explains it:

> Since you have been raised to new life with Christ, set your sights on the realities of heaven, where Christ sits in the place of honor at God's right hand. Think about the things of heaven, not the things of earth. For you died to this life, and your real life is hidden with Christ in God.

You have died to this life, and your real life is hidden with Christ in God. The position of Christ, according to Ephesians 1, is far above any ruler or authority or power or leader or anything else, not only in this world but also in the world to come. He is supreme over all. And we are seated with Him, hidden in Him. There is a divine council in the heavenly realm where Christ is seated, and we are seated there with Him.

No wonder the enemy fights so hard to keep us prayerless, because he knows our position. The enemy is under Christ's feet, which means he is also under our feet. Although we live on earth, we are seated in heavenly places.

When you understood your position, your prayers will change. So many Christians think they are praying up to heaven and that the enemy blocks them. But that is not what is happening. Yes, we live on earth, but we are also seated in heavenly places. This is portrayed in Ephesians chapter 6: "For we do not wrestle against flesh and blood, but against principalities, against powers, against the rulers of the darkness of this age, against spiritual hosts of wickedness *in the heavenly places*" (Ephesians 6:12 NKJV, emphasis added).

Remember, your position in Christ is far above all of that. The enemy wants you to believe that you are under him. But you are not, because you are hidden in Christ, seated with Him in heavenly places. Your position in Christ is far above, so your prayers are heard in a different place.

This is why the angel told Daniel that his prayer had been answered the day he prayed it, although the enemy blocked the answer for a time (see Daniel 10). The answer was released the day Daniel prayed because of Daniel's position in the heavenly places. But when God released the answer, it had to get through the things that were beneath. The principality was trying to stop the answer from going down; it was not trying to keep a prayer from going up.

What is this heavenly council? We see the heavenly council not only in Psalm 82 (quoted at the beginning of this chapter), but again in the book of Job: "One day the members of the heavenly court came to present themselves before the

LORD, and the Accuser, Satan, came with them. 'Where have you come from?' the LORD asked Satan" (Job 1:6–7).

In other words, Satan was not really supposed to be there. He was eavesdropping. The members of the heavenly court came together for a meeting, and Satan showed up, like, "Hey, it's been a while. What's going on?" (This is huge when you understand what is happening. The council in the heavenly realm is where the enemy accuses you, as I will soon show you.)

The heavenly council is mentioned again in Job 2:1–2:

> One day the members of the heavenly court came again to present themselves before the LORD, and the Accuser, Satan, came with them. "Where have you come from?" the LORD asked Satan.
>
> Satan answered the LORD, "I have been patrolling the earth, watching everything that's going on."

We have established that there is a meeting in the heavenlies in which the things of the earth are discussed. Now let's see how all of this works.

A Vision of Heaven's Council

We read in 2 Chronicles 18 about Ahab, the king of Israel, who asked Jehoshaphat, the king of Judah, if he would join him in going to war against Ramoth Gilead. Jehoshaphat said his people would be with Ahab in the war, but he asked the king of Israel to inquire of the Lord before going into battle.

Four hundred prophets told the kings God would give them victory in the battle. But Jehoshaphat pressed for further confirmation and asked if there was another prophet of whom they could inquire. Ahab told him about the prophet Micaiah, but he said, "I hate him. He never prophesies anything but trouble for me!" (verse 7). But Jehoshaphat insisted that they seek the word of the Lord through Micaiah:

> Then he came to the king; and the king said to him, "Micaiah, shall we go to war against Ramoth Gilead, or shall I refrain?"
>
> And he said, "Go and prosper, and they shall be delivered into your hand!"
>
> So the king said to him, "How many times shall I make you swear that you tell me nothing but the truth in the name of the LORD?"
>
> Then he said, "I saw all Israel scattered on the mountains, as sheep that have no shepherd. And the LORD said, 'These have no master. Let each return to his house in peace.'" [In other words, Micaiah prophesied that Ahab was going to die.] And the king of Israel said to Jehoshaphat, "Did I not tell you he would not prophesy good concerning me, but evil?"
>
> 2 Chronicles 18:14–17 NKJV

This is where the story gets really interesting.

> Then Micaiah said, "Therefore hear the word of the LORD: I saw the LORD sitting on His throne, and all the host of heaven standing on His right hand and His left. And the LORD said, 'Who will persuade Ahab king of Israel to go up, that he may fall at Ramoth Gilead?' So one spoke in this manner, and another spoke in that manner. Then a spirit came forward and stood before the LORD, and said, 'I will persuade him.'

The LORD said to him, 'In what way?' So he said, 'I will go
out and be a lying spirit in the mouth of all his prophets.'
And the LORD said, 'You shall persuade him and also prevail;
go out and do so.' Therefore look! The LORD has put a lying
spirit in the mouth of these prophets of yours, and the LORD
has declared disaster against you."

2 Chronicles 18:18–22 NKJV

What did Micaiah see? He looked and saw the council of
heaven. And what was happening there? Spirits were talking
to spirits about the affairs of the earth. This is what is happening in the heavenly council. But remember, God never
intended to have divine orchestration without human participation. So what Micaiah the prophet saw happening in
the heavenly council was God saying, "Who's going to persuade Ahab to go into battle?" And one spirit says this, and
another spirit says that, and then a spirit came forward and
stood before the Lord and said, "I will persuade him." And
the spirit volunteered to become a lying spirit in the mouths
of the prophets. The Lord said, "Go and do it."

Now, let's pause here, because you are probably thinking,
"Wait a minute. What is going on? A holy spirit of God
actually became a lying spirit?" No; let me explain. In all
likelihood, this was another instance of Satan slipping into
the council of God. Look back at that account in the book
of Job about the council of heaven that came together. Who
also came? Satan. He was not invited, but he showed up and
God permitted him to speak.

The devil is a liar (see John 8:44 and Revelation 12:9).
What God is really saying when He tells him to lie to the
prophets is that since lying is the only thing Satan knows how

to do, he will succeed at lying. God's wisdom is ultimate and infinite. He knows how to use the devil for His glory. Our God has all power and all wisdom, and if He needs to use the enemy to accomplish His goals, He will do that.

Four hundred false prophets had prophesied victory, but when Micaiah got a peek into the council of heaven and saw the spirits talking, he knew that they had a lying spirit in their mouths. In verse 23 (NKJV), Zedekiah, son of Chenaanah, slapped Micaiah on the cheek and said, "Which way did the spirit from the LORD go from me to speak to you?" In other words, he was saying, "How dare you call me a liar?" And Micaiah simply said, "Look, I know what I saw."

And, of course, Micaiah's words proved to be correct. Ahab was killed in battle.

Taking a closer look at the council, it seems amazing not only that the fallen spirit, Satan, has a voice there, but also that God allowed a human to overhear the proceedings so that he could tell others. It seems to be the case that God includes righteous human beings in the council.

But, of course, righteous human beings are hard to find. Righteousness is rare upon the earth, and it was especially scarce under the Old Covenant. Today we live under the New Covenant, under which righteousness has been imputed by our faith in Christ.[1]

It appears that God considered Micaiah to be righteous.

Intercession—Your Voice in the Heavenly Council

Remember, God never intends to have divine orchestration without human participation. The human participation is called prayer. And not just prayer, but *intercessory* prayer.

There is a difference. Humankind participates in the council of heaven by means of intercession. We see this in Genesis 18, when Abraham interceded for the wicked city of Sodom, asking God to save the city if even ten righteous people could be found.

Nations such as the United States have what is called a representative government. The electorate in each state sends someone to represent their needs in Congress. Similarly, the Church is a global body, and the local church is the representative of the region where it is located. Have you ever thought about it this way?

Humankind participates in the council of heaven by means of intercession.

During election seasons, a candidate will run negative political ads claiming that his or her opponent does not show up for work and misses important votes. What those negative ads are actually saying is that the person failed to represent his or her constituents appropriately. The same thing happens when churches are prayerless: We end up with regions that are not represented when the heavenly council is discussing their area because their seat at the table is vacant.

You are seated with Christ in heavenly places (see Ephesians 2:6). When decisions are being made concerning your geographical region, God wants to know what you have to say about it. Intercession is your way of having a conversation with God about particular things that are happening on the earth. He wants people who will speak up for the region they are in.

Often, God will divulge His plans within His council. Remember what He said regarding Abraham:

"Should I hide my plan from Abraham? . . . For Abraham will certainly become a great and mighty nation, and all the nations of the earth will be blessed through him. I have singled him out so that he will direct his sons and their families to keep the way of the LORD by doing what is right and just. Then I will do for Abraham all that I have promised."

Genesis 18:17–19

Whom was God talking to? He was talking to the council. We can see that He was declaring a day in the future when everyone who believes like Abraham will have a seat on the council. A day would be coming when God would extend righteousness to the people who believe in His Son. And He could not *not* include Abraham, because He was going to extend righteousness to the whole of humanity who believed as Abraham did. In addition, God singled Abraham out so that he would direct his descendants to keep the way of the Lord by doing what is right.

So in verse 20, the Lord told Abraham, "I have heard a great outcry from Sodom and Gomorrah, because their sin is so flagrant." Who made the outcry if there was no one righteous there? It had to be the spirits in the council if there was no one righteous in the cities. They must have been saying, "God, You better do something about this city on the earth because there is no righteousness in it; they are wicked and evil."

As the council was meeting about Sodom and Gomorrah, God told Abraham,

"I am going down to see if their actions are as wicked as I have heard. If not, I want to know." The other men turned

and headed toward Sodom, but the LORD remained with
Abraham. Abraham approached him and said, "Will you
sweep away both the righteous and the wicked?"

Genesis 18:21–23

Here a man is talking to God about His will concerning
a region.

I tell you: If you will get this, it will change the way you
pray. So many Christians think we are praying down here
from a feeble position, trying to get our petitions up to
heaven so maybe God will tell us something. But God is
saying, "I want to talk to you about what is happening on
the earth."

Abraham begins to bargain with God: "Listen, suppose
You find fifty righteous people living in Sodom. Will You still
sweep it away and not spare it for their sakes?" (see Genesis
18:24). This is intercession. Abraham regards God's decision
to destroy Sodom, and he dares to engage in a discussion
about it. He knows that God is the supreme Judge, but he
also recognizes that, since God is talking with him about
this, he is allowed to respond.

He told the Lord, "Surely you would not do such a thing,
destroying the righteous along with the wicked. Why, you
would be treating the righteous and the wicked exactly the
same! Surely you wouldn't do that! Should not the Judge
of all the earth do what is right?" (Genesis 18:25 NLT). The
Lord agreed to spare the city for the sake of fifty righteous
people (see verse 26), but of course there were not that
many righteous people in Sodom. Abraham continued to
intercede for Sodom until he had gone from fifty to forty
to thirty and finally to just ten righteous people. (Abraham

was interceding for Sodom, but he was also interceding on behalf of his family because his nephew, Lot, had settled there. Although he recognized that God intended to judge Sodom, Abraham was saying, "There is somebody I love in the city, so I am asking You not to destroy the city. Hear me, because there is somebody in the city I want to save. Have mercy, I am asking You.")

What did God do in response to Abraham's persistent intercession? He could not find even ten righteous people in Sodom, but He did save Lot and his family before He destroyed the city.

Pray without Ceasing

The apostle Paul urges us to "pray without ceasing" (1 Thessalonians 5:17 NKJV). Why does he say this? Because of the heavenly council. We are seated in heavenly places with Christ Jesus, and there are things being discussed concerning the regions we live in, and God intends for us to be involved in those discussions. The ministry of intercession is not reserved for a special group of people. It is for everybody who has been seated in heavenly places with Christ Jesus—and that means all of us.

This means that if you do not show up for the council, you are making the blood of Jesus less powerful in your life. And when you do show up, you are not there in that council simply so that you can discuss your wish list. Consider this: Whenever a politician in a representative government uses his or her position for personal gain, we call that corruption. In a similar way, why would you ever use your seat on the council for personal gain?

Your seat in the council has been paid for by the blood of Jesus. You are there in the heavenly realm where things are being discussed about your city, and all you want to talk about is getting a new house or a new car? All you want to interject into the conversation is your desire for a spouse or a better-paying job? That is not the best way to use the authority you were given when God seated you in heavenly places with Christ Jesus.

Remember, Jesus said to seek first the Kingdom of God and His righteousness, and all these things would be added (see Matthew 6:33). Satan wants you worried about your life and how your needs will be met. But God wants you focused on His Kingdom, because if you will do that, everything else will fall into place.

The enemy wants you off-focus, so you will not use your seat and your voice to bring about change in your region. He understands that the things happening in the heavenly council very much affect what happens in your local city council. So he would rather have you spend your time asking God for personal provision and protection and restoration instead of looking beyond your own immediate desires.

We as the Church have not been walking in the kind of power and authority we have been given, because we do not realize that real change happens in the heavenly council. What we do is tell people they need to bombard their city council. It is not that God does not want to put some Christians in local or even national politics. But those who are not called to the civic arena are called to another arena—a heavenly arena that affects every facet of what happens in the earth.

When the things of heaven influence the things of earth, you will hear statements such as these: "Well, we have never done that before, but we will make an exception for you," or "We do not know exactly why we are doing this, but it seems agreeable," or "This is just a new idea that came to us." This is called heavenly favor. When you pray for favor, this is what the answers to your prayer may sound like: "This is something new," and "We have never given this to anybody before," or "We have never structured a loan like this before," or "We have never written off a building like this before." The public officials do not realize that the heavenly council is affecting their earthly decisions.

Never forget that what we can see on this earth is not all there is to it. Not even close. We are residents of earth, but our citizenship is in heaven. And no matter what the accuser says, we belong with Christ in heavenly places. God did not make a mistake when He gave us the access we have. We belong in our seat in the council, which is a topic we will explore in the next chapter.

PRAYER

My God and King, oh, how incredible it is to realize that I too can sit on Your council, and that my voice will be heard there even as I pray here on earth. Illuminate this reality to my understanding, because it is far too great for me. My participation in Your council will not be impeded as long as I dwell in Your presence. With joyful acknowledgment of Jesus as the One who saves, Amen.

7

Residents of Earth, Citizens of Heaven

But we are citizens of heaven, where the Lord Jesus Christ lives. And we are eagerly waiting for him to return as our Savior.

Philippians 3:20

The key to answered prayer is the place from which you ask. That statement has a dual reality. Here on earth, we are abiding in Him by our intentional decisions to make Christ our number one priority. Yet at the same time we are citizens of heaven.

Colossians 3:3 says we died to this life and our "real life is hidden with Christ in God." And Ephesians 2:6 tells us that we are seated with Christ in heavenly places. This means that we are residents of earth and also citizens of heaven.

This is one of the reasons we call funerals home-going services; we know this earth is not our home. We believe that we will be delivered from our bodies, which are mere shells that will turn into dust. We will receive glorified bodies on the Day of Resurrection, but our current bodies will turn to dust. Our bodies are not our homes; heaven is. The sickness that touches your body does not touch your spirit because your body is not the permanent home of your spirit.

We are residents here on earth, but also citizens there in heaven: We see this in Paul's letter to the church of Philippi: "But we are citizens of heaven, where the Lord Jesus Christ lives. And we are eagerly waiting for him to return as our Savior" (Philippians 3:20). The verse reads this way in the Passion Translation: "But we are a colony of heaven on earth as we cling tightly to our life-giver, the Lord Jesus Christ."

To understand why Paul would write something like that, we have to understand his audience. They would know what Paul meant because Philippi was a Roman colony and its residents, though physically located in Macedonia, were citizens of Rome. Paul was writing to a people who would completely understand what it means to be citizens of one place while residents of another.

The Philippians knew exactly what it would mean to live upon the earth yet dress like a citizen of heaven. They understood what it would mean to live upon the earth yet speak as a citizen of heaven, to engage in the pleasures of being a citizen of heaven and not earth, to live by the laws of heaven as well as the laws of earth. (Even though we live by a higher law, we still obey the laws of earth.) The Philippians understood what it meant to worship the God of heaven and not the gods of the earth.

To be a citizen of heaven is to focus your attention on God and not the god of this nation, which is money. You cannot worship both. Jesus is clear about that; He says you cannot serve both God and money (see Matthew 6:24). You can be devoted to only one, and you will despise the other.

Shifting Paradigms

A *paradigm* is a set of concepts or a theoretical framework—simply put, a way of thinking. Therefore, a *paradigm shift* means a change to a way of thinking.

We need a paradigm shift in how we view prayer. Most of us have been taught all our lives that we are down here on earth trying to get our prayers through to God in heaven. We are down here hoping that He hears us, and those who have a little more faith are more likely to get answers. But that is not what is happening.

You are seated with Christ in heavenly places. You are living on the earth, and you are simultaneously a citizen of heaven. You are seated in heavenly places with Christ. Because of what Jesus did for you on the cross, you have been given unhindered access to God. You have a seat on the divine council, which means your prayers are heard in two places at the same time. Not only that, but your prayers are *said* in two places at the same time.

You have a seat on the divine council, which means your prayers are heard in two places at the same time.

In Christian circles we hear about this all the time, but we do not live it. We hear that we have unhindered access to God, but when we need Him, we approach Him as if we think we are bothering Him. We do not actually live as if we have unhindered access to God.

In reality, when we pray, our prayers are taking place in two places at the same time. The enemy works day and night to convince us that our prayers are not working, or more specifically, that they are not penetrating the heavenly realm. However, even the prayers we cannot seem to phrase correctly are not only penetrating the heavenly places; they are being spoken in those heavenly places at the very same moment that they are spoken on earth.

Think about it: Christ is seated above all powers, and everything is under His feet. You are living on earth, but in your spirit you are seated with Him, hidden in Him. That is why, when you pray on earth, your prayers are audible in heaven.

As we have said before, people like to blame the powers of hell for stopping their prayers. But the powers of hell cannot do this; all they can do is delay the answer.

When Jesus taught us to pray, "Our Father, who art in heaven. Hallowed be Your name. Your Kingdom come. Your will be done on earth as it already is in heaven" (see Matthew 6:9–10), the phrase "as it already is in heaven" tells us that in heaven, His will is already done. We will look more closely at this truth in the next chapter, but for now this is what I want you to see: The answers are already there. There is not a question you can ask that God does not have an answer for. When you pray about something, God does not have to rush around in heaven trying to figure out how He is going to make something happen for you. It is already done. The answer is already there. What are you asking for then? You are asking for it to be manifested on the earth.

The prayer Jesus taught us is saying this: Let the earth reflect what is already happening in heaven. Let us see in the natural what we have already seen in the spirit. Let the earth mirror what has been done already in heaven.

Everything we need is already done, already fulfilled, already accomplished. When we see God do something miraculous, there is always more where that came from. When we see somebody get up out of a wheelchair, there is more of that. God does not have a limited supply. It is not as if He is saying to us, "Now you can add that to your 'been there, done that' checklist and remember those times fondly." No, there will be more where that came from.

When you go to a store and you do not see what you are looking for, you can go to a clerk and ask if they have any more. And often the clerk will go back into a storeroom, where there is an abundant supply of the item you are looking for. They have more. That is like heaven. Heaven is a storehouse for earth's answers.

The Lord asked Job if he had visited "the storehouses of the snow or seen the storehouses of hail" (Job 38:22). Then He said, "I have reserved them as weapons for the time of trouble, for the day of battle and war" (verse 23). In other words, "I have a storehouse of answers ready for when you need them." Heaven is like a storehouse of answers for earth's prayers.

He Has Already Provided

As we saw in the previous chapter, there is a divine council in the heavenly realm where Jesus is seated, and we are seated there with Him. The reason the enemy fights you so hard to keep you prayerless is because if he can keep you prayerless, he can keep your seat on the council unoccupied and your voice silenced. One of the easiest ways he has for keeping us silent is by getting us to worry about our provision.

As we already discussed, Jesus addressed this clearly:

"Therefore I say to you, do not worry about your life, what you will eat or what you will drink; nor about your body, what you will put on. Is not life more than food and the body more than clothing? Look at the birds of the air, for they neither sow nor reap nor gather into barns; yet your heavenly Father feeds them. Are you not of more value than they? Which of you by worrying can add one cubit to his stature?

"So why do you worry about clothing? Consider the lilies of the field, how they grow: they neither toil nor spin; and yet I say to you that even Solomon in all his glory was not arrayed like one of these. Now if God so clothes the grass of the field, which today is, and tomorrow is thrown into the oven, will He not much more clothe you, O you of little faith?"

Matthew 6:25–30 NKJV

He is saying, "Listen, I do not want you to have a misplaced focus. Do not worry about food or clothing or other provisions. You do not need to worry about those things because you are a council member. You are a child of the Most High God. I am telling you that you do not need to sit there talking about your needs, because that will keep you from talking about the matters of real importance. I am telling you not to fall for the enemy's ploy; he wants to keep you focused on small things so you will forget to bring up the big things when you pray."

If you focus your attention on God's Kingdom, it becomes your priority, your pursuit and your desire. Soon you will notice that everything else you need is taken care of.

It is as if the enemy is trying to give you spiritual ADD (attention deficit disorder), distracting you with financial struggles or your kids or haters on the internet. He is aware of your position in God's high council, but he wants you to forget about it.

> **The enemy is trying to give you spiritual ADD.... He is aware of your position in God's high council, but he wants you to forget about it.**

Lord of Hosts

One of the descriptors of our God is the "Lord of Hosts." See, for instance, Psalm 46:11 (NKJV). The Passion Translation and *The Message* render that phrase "the GOD [or Commander, or Lord] of the angel [or heaven's] armies." This is not a reference to many gods. The Lord of Hosts is the singular God who created all other beings that serve at His pleasure. He is the Lord over hosts of angelic beings. They all report to Him.

Other Scriptures refer to angelic beings in a variety of ways: as the "host of heaven" (1 Kings 22:19 NKJV), angel armies (Isaiah 5:7 MSG) and even the "sons of God" (Genesis 6:2). Every time you read in Scripture about a gathering of celestial beings or "sons of God," that is actually a council meeting.

Zechariah 1 speaks of a vision God gave the prophet:

> In a vision during the night, I saw a man sitting on a red horse that was standing among some myrtle trees in a small valley.

Behind him were riders on red, brown, and white horses. I asked the angel who was talking with me, "My lord, what do these horses mean?"

"I will show you," the angel replied. The rider standing among the myrtle trees then explained, "They are the ones the LORD has sent out to patrol the earth." Then the other riders reported to the angel of the LORD, who was standing among the myrtle trees, "We have been patrolling the earth, and the whole earth is at peace."

Zechariah 1:8–11

One of the ways we know this heavenly council exists is because of passages like this one, where God allowed the prophets of old to peer into the council meeting. In the last chapter, we examined a reference to the heavenly council found in 2 Chronicles 18. Here I want to draw your attention to two more instances in Scripture where God allowed prophets to peer into and see the council of heaven:

I watched as thrones were put in place and the Ancient One sat down to judge. His clothing was as white as snow, his hair like purest wool. He sat on a fiery throne with wheels of blazing fire, and a river of fire was pouring out, flowing from his presence. Millions of angels ministered to him; many millions stood to attend him. Then the court began its session, and the books were opened.

Daniel 7:9–10

What was Daniel seeing? A council, which is also known as the heavenly court.

In the year that King Uzziah died, I saw the Lord sitting on a throne, high and lifted up, and the train of His robe filled the temple. Above it stood seraphim; each one had six wings: with two he covered his face, with two he covered his feet, and with two he flew. And one cried to another and said: "Holy, holy, holy is the LORD of hosts; the whole earth is full of His glory!" And the posts of the door were shaken by the voice of him who cried out, and the house was filled with smoke.

Isaiah 6:1–4 NKJV

This is probably the most famous vision of the heavenly council. Notice that God chose to speak to Isaiah and allowed the prophet to answer as he looked in on the council. This is because God never intended to have divine orchestration without human participation.

You Are Chosen

Do you get the picture? Believers are operating simultaneously in two places. We pray, worship and give to God in two places at the same time.

There is probably no better illustration of this than Zechariah 3:1–7:

Then the angel showed me Jeshua the high priest standing before the angel of the LORD. The Accuser, Satan, was there at the angel's right hand, making accusations against Jeshua. And the LORD said to Satan, "I, the LORD, reject your accusations, Satan. Yes, the LORD, who has chosen Jerusalem, rebukes you. This man is like a burning stick that has been snatched from the fire."

Jeshua's clothing was filthy as he stood there before the angel. So the angel said to the others standing there, "Take off his filthy clothes." And turning to Jeshua he said, "See, I have taken away your sins, and now I am giving you these fine new clothes."

Then I said, "They should also place a clean turban on his head." So they put a clean priestly turban on his head and dressed him in new clothes while the angel of the LORD stood by.

Then the angel of the LORD spoke very solemnly to Jeshua and said, "This is what the LORD of Heaven's Armies says: If you follow my ways and carefully serve me, then you will be given authority over my Temple and its courtyards. I will let you walk among these others standing here."

Zechariah 3:1–7

In this passage, the prophet is seeing the divine council. Just as we saw in the first two chapters of Job, which we discussed in chapter 6, the accuser is there. Here he is at the right hand of the priest Jeshua, accusing him.

Now, this is critical to understand. Jeshua is the high priest, which means he is not standing there for himself. He represents all the people of Israel and is offering sacrifices on their behalf to remove their sin. Standing there in his priestly duty as a representative of the people, Jeshua is supposed to be clean. But the Scripture says in verse 3 that his clothes were filthy and Satan, the accuser, could not wait to point that out, saying, "They do not deserve forgiveness." He is demanding justice. But God chooses to show Jeshua mercy.

Satan the accuser was correct in saying that Jeshua was guilty. He wanted God to remove His hand from the people of Israel and kill them because the Law said that if they were dirty, then they should be dead. It was as if he was telling God, "This is the cleanest one? This is Your chosen people? They are filthy!"

But God said, "I rebuke you, because I chose them." This is all-important. Many of us are afraid to pray because we do not think we belong in the heavenly council. But do you see who speaks up for you? God Himself says, "I rebuke you, Satan. I rebuke you, accuser, because I chose them."

You are chosen. You are not perfect, but you are chosen. You are not spotless on your own, but you are chosen. You might have messed up yesterday, but you are chosen. If that does not make you want to shout, I don't know what will!

You Belong on the Council

Throughout the history of Israel, the people had an on-again, off-again relationship with God, even though He always kept His word to them. The enemy continually attempted to deal with the Israelites by using nations to oppress them, and this is why he showed up at this council.

When God said, "I rebuke these accusations because I chose them," He also said, "Is this not the branch that was snatched from the fire?" In other words, He was saying, "Listen, I understand that they turned from Me. I understand that they were in captivity, but I have chosen them." Notice that God was the One who rebuked the accuser. This is because He was the One who chose.

The enemy is accusing us, God's remnant, the ones who are trying to live right. Satan is saying we are unholy and unworthy. He says, "They do not deserve healing. They do not deserve revival. They do not deserve to even have their prayers heard, much less answered. They do not deserve Your goodness. They do not deserve Your favor. They are dirty and unfit to be used."

Our guilty conscience comes from what we hear being said about us, as the accuser states his case in the council. You do not know why you have a guilty conscience on the earth. You may be just walking down the street, going into the grocery store, when suddenly you feel guilty. Or you may be trying to go into the presence of God during worship, and all you can think about are all the things you did wrong and how unworthy you are. This is because while you are here on the earth minding your business, the accuser is up in the council saying, "They do not deserve it. They are guilty." Your guilty conscience comes from what you are overhearing.

You are experiencing what is called "critic's math," in which a thousand compliments plus one negative comment equals one negative comment. This is what happens when the devil accuses us. We let our guilt erase God's promise.

This is why it is so important that you study the Word. The accuser is constantly doing his job, and we need to do ours. If we do not, we will not have anything with which to counteract what we are overhearing.

Day and night you may be hearing a list of your sins, and it may be making you toss and turn in your bed. But when you understand what Jesus Christ has done for you, you can go to sleep in peace. Then you can lift up your hands freely, without anger or doubting. Then you can boldly approach the throne of God, because you know that the things the accuser is saying are not true.

You Deserve Your Seat

While the accuser is busy saying what we do and do not deserve, let me remind you what our God does for us. First, He says, "I chose them." Tell yourself right now, "I am chosen by God." Let that sink in. Get that into your spirit.

The accuser then says, "Their clothes are filthy." God says, "I am going to remove their ragged clothes and give them expensive clothes." This represents not only the mercy of God, but the grace of God, because the mercy of God is replacing your dirty clothes with garments you could never earn or buy and do not even deserve. And He is saying, "This is how I want you to stand in My presence." He wants you to stand there knowing you are forgiven and redeemed, and that you belong.

At this point in the passage, the prophet speaks up. He has been watching the council and he says, "They should put a clean turban on his head." So they put a clean turban on his head. What is written on the turban is "Holy to the Lord." To be holy means to be set apart. So God responds to our filth and unworthiness with His mercy and grace and by setting us apart for His purpose. He covers us with what we could not buy and did not deserve and then He covers our head with something that proclaims, "You are set apart for Me."

In the final instruction of the angel of the Lord (verse 7), Jeshua was urged to follow the Lord's ways carefully. If he did so, he would be given authority over "my Temple and its courtyards" (which means the earth), and he would be allowed to "walk among these others standing here" (which means the heavenly council). Like Jeshua, we too can be residents of earth and citizens of heaven at the same time.

So how does this work? I have one word for you: Jesus. *He* is how this works. The next verse in Zechariah 3 underlines this: "Listen to me, O Jeshua the high priest, and all you other priests. You are symbols of things to come. Soon I am going to bring my servant, the Branch" (Zechariah 3:8). Who is the Branch? The Branch is Jesus.

Remember Jesus' words: "I am the true grapevine, and my Father is the gardener. He cuts off every branch of mine that doesn't produce fruit, and he prunes the branches that do bear fruit so they will produce even more" (John 15:1–2).

When you feel unworthy of your authority in Christ, you are overhearing the accuser. But remember what Jesus did:

> We can boldly enter heaven's Most Holy Place because of the blood of Jesus. By his death, Jesus opened a new and life-giving way through the curtain into the Most Holy Place. And since we have a great High Priest who rules over God's house, let us go right into the presence of God with sincere hearts fully trusting him. For our guilty consciences have been sprinkled with Christ's blood to make us clean, and our bodies have been washed with pure water.
>
> Hebrews 10:19–22

We have a great high priest—not Jeshua but *Yeshua*, Jesus. In Him, there is no filth. In Him, there is no dirt. He is clean, and He has imputed His purity to us. Our great High Priest rules over God's house. Because of this, we can go before God without guilt or shame.

Your guilty conscience has been washed clean. You can tell the enemy, "Whatever you say, I can't hear you because my conscience has been wiped clean by the blood of Jesus!"

When you know what God says about you, you do not have to pay any attention to the lies of the accuser. You know your conscience has been sprinkled with Christ's blood to make you clean, and you can be confident that you deserve your seat on the council!

PRAYER

My Lord, I rejoice in my dual citizenship! Even as I live within my country on earth, keep me from squandering the benefits of my citizenship in heaven, because that is my place of permanent citizenship. At the same time, I pray that Your Kingdom will invade my place on earth and that the day will come when the whole world will be pervaded and purified according to Your sovereign will. You are the King of kings, and Jesus is Your high priest, who ushers me into Your presence. Come, Lord Jesus! Amen.

8

As It Is in Heaven

"In this manner, therefore, pray: Our Father in heaven, hallowed be Your name. Your kingdom come. Your will be done on earth as it is in heaven."

Matthew 6:9–10 NKJV

You have probably heard many definitions of prayer, but here is another one for you to consider: Prayer is the access point by which the realities of the invisible world, the Kingdom of God, enter the visible world, which is the earth.

When we pray, we lay hold of what is already a reality in the heavens and call it to manifest here on the earth. Prayer is a supernatural transaction that affects natural things. For this reason, the way we deal with things is by prayer; we should not try to deal with needs by earthly means.

However, in order to pray effectively, you must first understand the access and authority that you have been given, and the place you are praying from. This means that you have to learn to think differently; you have to shift your paradigm.

Naturally, oftentimes we think we already know a thing, especially if we have been saved a long time. But when God's Word shows us something different from what we have always believed, His Word is not wrong—we are. It is up to us to adjust our thinking and our lives. If what we were taught is not biblical, we must surrender our old way of doing things to the Word of God. For example, as we saw in chapter 4, there are those who will blame the devil for unanswered prayers when in reality, it is offense, unforgiveness or discord that is keeping their prayers from being answered.

Another important paradigm shift we discussed in chapter 5 has to do with understanding our true identity in Christ, which in turn informs the way we pray. When Jesus taught His disciples how to pray, He started out like this: "In this manner, therefore, pray: Our Father in heaven, hallowed be Your name. Your Kingdom come. Your will be done on earth as it is in heaven" (Matthew 6:9–10 NKJV). In this prayer, He referred to "our Father." God is not only Jesus' Father, but also our Father. Knowing this confirms our identity. We do not have to strive to become God's sons and daughters; that is who we are already. And as Bishop Tony Miller of the Destiny Fellowship of Churches once said, "Our identity informs our activity. Our activity does not determine our identity."

You Are Not a Stranger

Knowing who you are should affect the way you pray. When you go into the place of prayer, you are not going in as a stranger. You do not need to introduce yourself to God. You do not have to say, "God, it has been a long time since I have been here, and I know I should be praying more." No, because He sees you as a son or daughter, you do not ever have to introduce yourself to God, just as you never have to introduce yourself to the people who raised you. Some of us are spending time in prayer trying to build up credibility with God when we are already His.

I (Pastor Caleb) have a two-year-old son, and even if he has made a mess in his diaper or in his room, he still runs to me because he knows whom he belongs to. In a similar way, our prayers will change when we are sure about who we are: sons and daughters of God. Then when we pray, "Our Father in heaven, hallowed be Your name. Your kingdom come. Your will be done on earth as it is in heaven," we can pray with confidence and authority.

Look again at that last part: "Your kingdom come. Your will be done *on earth as it is in heaven.*" Songs have been written around these simple lines: "Your kingdom come. Your will be done on earth as it is in heaven." Yet many of us do not fully grasp the power of the statement.

When you ask for the Kingdom of heaven to come to earth, you are actually saying, "God, it is already finished. Now let it be on earth as it is in heaven. God, what You have already done in heaven, I want to see on the earth." We want to see the earth catch up with heaven.

I am pointing this out to reinforce the reality of our heavenly access. Think of it this way: Have you ever been welcomed to stay at someone's house with the words, "Make yourself at home; you're family"? Now, most of us will nod our heads, but not take it to heart. However, if I hear that, I might say, "Are you sure?" Because I love to eat, and if you give me access to your family fridge, you may have to stock up on groceries!

Here is what I mean. When I first moved here from Canada, I was living with Pastor William for a few months while I was waiting for my beautiful fiancée, who is now my wife, to come to the United States so we could get married. Pastor William said, "You're family, bro. Whatever is in the fridge is yours. It's fine." After I had been at their house for maybe a few weeks, I was beginning to settle in and get comfortable in Florida.

Pastor William is a wonderful cook, and one night for dinner he made this big spaghetti dish with cheese layered on the top. I probably had three servings; it was so good. Finally, I reached the point where I was like, *Okay, I need to chill. I know I have access, but it is time to just relax.* I was not really full, but I figured I needed to stop. Later, in the middle of the night, I woke up and I was hungry. Now, most people might have settled for a bowl of cereal. But I remembered that massive dish of leftover spaghetti in the fridge, and I thought, *My Lord, You are so good to me!* So I ate all the leftover spaghetti, and I went back to bed with a smile on my face.

The next morning, I got a text from Pastor William. He was like, "Hey, bro, we're looking for the spaghetti. Do you know where it is?"

I didn't even blink. I was like, "Oh, yeah, bro. I ate the rest of it."

He's like, "You ate *all* of it? Bro, my wife and I were going to feed the whole family with what you ate in one sitting."

But I had felt welcome to eat my fill of his spaghetti because he had told me to make myself at home. Needless to say, I was embarrassed. But all I had done was simply taken advantage of the access I had been given.

Access Granted

We may receive with our minds the idea that we have free access to the things of the Spirit, but if many of us are honest, we truly do not pray or live as if we have been given full and free access into heavenly places. Still, just as a host may repeat, "Make yourself at home," often God will repeat a word. He will remind you of the truth, as the writer of the book of Hebrews did: "And now we are brothers and sisters in God's family because of the blood of Jesus, and he welcomes us to come right into the most holy sanctuary in the heavenly realm—boldly and with no hesitation" (Hebrews 10:19 TPT).

You and I are welcome in the heavenly realm because of the blood of Jesus. He has given us a way to approach God. For just as the veil was torn in two, Jesus' body was torn open to give us free and fresh access to Him. And since we have a magnificent High Priest—that being Jesus—to welcome us into God's house, we come closer to God and approach Him with an open heart, fully convinced that nothing will keep us at a distance from Him. Our hearts have been sprinkled with blood to remove impurity, and we have been freed from an accusing conscience. We are clean, unstained and presentable to God inside and out. Even when we feel we do not deserve God's love and goodness, we have permission to enter into the heavenly council. The blood of Jesus has opened the way. You and I have access to the presence of God in worship, and we can enter into the place of prayer to commune with Him.

Instead of coming into His presence ruminating on something that happened last night or the way you dishonored your spouse, doubting yourself and thinking that God must be angry with you, you can come boldly before Him, entirely because of Jesus' sacrifice on the cross two thousand years ago.

You do not have to be afraid to lift your hands in worship, no matter what you have done. That is because when God looks at you, He sees the blood of Jesus. All He sees is the perfect sacrifice of Jesus. All He sees is the price that was paid. Jesus washed away your sins, and that removed the record of your wrongs. That is what forgiveness does. It removes the record of your wrongs. When you give your life to Christ, you no longer have a record of wrongs; there is nothing to look back to because God has forgiven you. The record has been destroyed.

In most countries, a person's criminal record is always held against him or her. Somehow, we think that God operates the same way. We think He is still holding some past blunder against us. But no, the forgiveness of Jesus is such that He tears up the legal papers and casts them into the sea. You have no criminal record. As soon as you repent, you gain free access to the presence of Jesus. If you find that you keep forgetting this, ask the Holy Spirit to help you change your paradigm. It will make all the difference.

You may have heard people say, "I am covered by the blood of Jesus," or, "I plead the blood of Jesus," or, "It is under the blood of Jesus." What they mean is that when Jesus said, "It is finished," every dysfunction and every curse was over. If you have surrendered your life to Jesus, your past sins are washed away as if you had never committed them (whether or not your heart has caught up with your head about it).

Having been given access to the Father by the blood of Jesus, you do not need to struggle, because in reality you are not at all far from God. As Pastor William tells worship leaders, "Our job is to make people aware of His nearness, because He is everywhere. He fills all space, all the time." So also, because the veil separating us from God has now been torn, nothing stands between us and Him, not even our guilty consciences. The blood of Jesus has made it possible for us to have open and free access.

Not only was our salvation purchased by the blood of Jesus, but so was our place in heaven. Our seat in heavenly places with Christ Jesus has been opened to us by His blood:

> But God is so rich in mercy, and he loved us so much, that even though we were dead because of our sins, he gave us life when he raised Christ from the dead. (It is only by God's grace that you have been saved!) For he raised us from the dead along with Christ and seated us with him in the heavenly realms because we are united with Christ Jesus.
>
> Ephesians 2:4–6

We are seated with Christ in heavenly places. When Jesus' blood was shed, our place in heaven was secured. So the moment you believed in Jesus, you were seated with Christ in heavenly places, and you received access into the heavenly council.

Our bodies are seated on the earth, because we dwell physically on the earth. But just as much, we are also seated in the realms of heaven.

We look expectantly for the return of Jesus, because then our mortal bodies will be transformed, and we will be given heavenly bodies that will function in the realms of the heavens permanently. But in the Spirit, we are already in heavenly places. We are not trying to get there. The moment we first believed in Jesus, He seated us there with Him.

Imagine yourself at the council, seated at the same table with Christ Jesus. You are not relegated to the kiddie table, but rather you are seated with Christ. So many Christians think there is still some sort of distance between them and God. I understand this. God is holy, and we feel so flawed. But "with Christ" means *with Christ*. And being seated with Christ means we have access to everything that Christ has.

Therefore, if Christ has all authority, that means we have access to all authority. If there is healing through the stripes that were laid on Jesus' back, that means we have access to that same healing. If there is deliverance and breakthrough found in Jesus Christ, then we have access to that deliverance because we are seated with Him.

Unfortunately, too many believers live by their flesh in the earthly realm. They live by their senses—by what they see, feel, hear, smell and touch. As a result, they feel limited. They are not living according to their heavenly citizenship.

While our bodies dwell in an earthly realm, our spirits as believers dwell in a heavenly realm. Behind our prayer, "Thy kingdom come. Thy will be done on earth as it is in heaven," we are saying, "I want the realities of heaven to take over." We want to live by the Spirit, as the apostle Paul admonishes us to do (see Galatians 5:16–26). When we live by the Spirit of God, we come into agreement with the culture we actually belong to—heaven.

The Benefits of Citizenship

Paul also wrote,

> Above all, you must live as citizens of heaven, conducting yourselves in a manner worthy of the Good News about Christ. Then, whether I come and see you again or only hear about you, I will know that you are standing together with one spirit and one purpose, fighting together for the faith, which is the Good News.
>
> Philippians 1:27

Our priority in life must be to live as citizens of heaven, even while everything on this earth endeavors to take our affection, our attention and our perspective away from the things of heaven. The forces of darkness do everything they can to keep us focused on the realities of earth. A believer who has forgotten his true citizenship and lives a life fully consumed by the affairs of the earth cannot and will not be effective in praying the will of heaven into the earth. This earth is not our home. Our permanent (and, dare I say, true) home is in heaven. Even while we continue to live within the customs and systems of this earth, we need to live with the mind-set, the attitude and the perspective of heaven. First and foremost, we are citizens of heaven.

In the same letter to the Philippians, Paul helps us understand this even more: "But we are citizens of heaven, where the Lord Jesus Christ lives. And we are eagerly waiting for him to return as our Savior" (Philippians 3:20). In other words, we have dual citizenship. Yes, we have a citizenship on the earth. We live here in our physical body, but in the realms of the spirit, in heavenly places, we also have full citizenship. And if that is where we reside as full citizens, then we do not have to be afraid to function there.

I am not afraid to function in my house. I will wear whatever I want, walk wherever I want and say whatever I want (as long as it honors the Lord). I can feel the same way about my place in heaven, and so can you.

Citizenship comes with benefits. A citizen is entitled to certain protections and advantages simply by having been born under a certain government (or because of having chosen to become naturalized). The privileges of citizenship here on the earth can give us good insight into how we should conduct ourselves when it comes to our citizenship in heaven.

Let's take a look at some of the benefits and privileges of citizenship.

Citizens Petition the Government for Protection

One of the privileges of my natural citizenship is that at any moment in time, as a citizen I can call the government of my nation to act on my behalf, especially in times when I need protection or to avoid danger. When you think of that in a spiritual context, it is worth shouting over. When you are in a place of trouble as David was when he was hounded by his enemies; or as the people of Israel were when they had been backed up against the Red Sea; or like Daniel in the lions' den; or like Shadrach, Meshach and Abednego in the fiery furnace, that is when you want to access the privileges of your citizenship in heaven. When you find yourself up against the wall, shipwrecked and beaten, or in a prison all night as Peter was, earthly authorities cannot help you. That is the time to ask the government of heaven to intervene in the affairs of the earth.

When you find yourself in trouble, that is not the time to call your senator; that is the time to call your King and say, "Jesus!" You have access to heaven, and protection and deliverance are a benefit of your citizenship.

Citizens Petition for Family Members to Become Citizens

In the United States and in many other countries, citizens are able to petition for other members of their family to become citizens. In a similar way, citizens of heaven can sit in the heavenly council and ask God to save their brothers and sisters. (We know that "brothers and sisters" include more than those in our immediate family.) You can petition heaven on behalf of anybody who is not saved and say, "I want these people to get in on what I have access to."

In addition, we can ask God to spare a city and to spare our families, as Abraham did in Genesis 18, because we want more people to come into the safety of the Kingdom.

This the place of intercession. Moses stepped forward to intercede for the people of Israel when God was about to wipe them out. Moses pleaded with God to spare the children of Israel. And God relented (see Exodus 33). Moses had obtained access to a position in heaven, to heavenly citizenship, and he made full use of it. From this same place of privilege, Abraham petitioned God for the welfare of Lot and his family. Never forget that you have access to heaven as a full citizen, one who can intercede on behalf of others.

Citizens Vote and Run for Public Office

A third benefit of earthly citizenship (at least in the United States and in many other countries) is that it gives you the ability to vote and run for public office. In other words, citizenship gives you a voice. With this voice, you are privileged to influence the affairs of the earth. When you go into the heavenly council in the place of prayer, you are voting. You are putting your mark in the box and having your say about what happens on the earth. It is as if you have submitted your ballot and said to your King, "Here is what I want to see change in my family/city/region. Please consider this."

When you have voting privileges and yet you do not exercise them, you not only fail to register your wishes, you also forfeit your opportunity to complain. Do not complain about the state of your city if you have not used your vote in the heavenly council. Do not complain about what you see in your family or in your school if you have neglected to use your vote.

Unfortunately, there are many believers who go through their lives complaining about the state of their lives. If we were honest, some of us use our voices only to complain. Such believers complain about their finances, their marriages, their bosses, the houses they live in, the pastors they have and so forth.

However, in reality these same believers actually have the power to cause circumstances to change on the earth by raising their voices in the realm of heaven.

Complaining is never the solution, but complaining when you have been given the power to affect the very thing you are complaining about is illogical and insulting when it is directed to the One who gave you a voice.

Stop complaining about the things you can change through prayer. Allow your holy frustration to drive you to your knees, and use your voice in heaven's council.

As a citizen of heaven, you have a voice on the heavenly council, and that voice is prayer. Prayer gives you a new perspective. Prayer gives you hope in a situation that seems hopeless.

Citizens Get Privileges and Benefits

Citizens of the United States (and other countries) have the opportunity to obtain federal jobs, grants and other government benefits that favor their well-being. In other words, citizens get favors that noncitizens cannot access.

People seem to recognize that believers have a similar kind of favor with God. Why do you think your unsaved co-workers ask you to pray for them? Because they know on some level that your relationship with God gives you access to something they do not feel they have access to. I am not saying that God does not hear the prayer of an unsaved person; after all, many of us were saved by prayers we prayed when we were yet unsaved. But people will look at you and presume that you have access to heaven. Do you see yourself the way they do?

When your co-workers ask you to pray for them, they are asking for access to the favor they see on your life. When everybody was getting laid off, they noticed that you still had peace. As a result, they want you to pray for them. There is something on you (and in you) that they want.

John the Baptist knew that everything comes from heaven:

Then Jesus and his disciples left Jerusalem and went into the Judean countryside. Jesus spent some time with them there, baptizing people. At this time John the Baptist was baptizing at Aenon, near Salim, because there was plenty of water there; and people kept coming to him for baptism. (This was before

John was thrown into prison.) A debate broke out between John's disciples and a certain Jew over ceremonial cleansing. So John's disciples came to him and said, "Rabbi, the man you met on the other side of the Jordan River, the one you identified as the Messiah, is also baptizing people. And everybody is going to him instead of coming to us." John replied, "No one can receive anything unless God gives it from heaven."

John 3:22–27

John told his disciples that what they were seeing was the favor that God had decided to bestow upon Jesus. In other words, what was happening was God's doing. Furthermore, this passage also carries the powerful connotation that no one can receive *anything*—healing, deliverance, breakthrough, life, salvation, grace—unless God gives it from heaven.

The blessing of the Lord comes from heaven. It does not come from us, nor does it come from the earth. Heaven is the warehouse or stock room of earth's answers, which also means that what you have seen on the earth already existed in heaven. By the same token, what you are asking to see on the earth already exists in heaven. When you pray, what you are saying is "I am accessing a resource that already exists, because I am in heavenly places. I am seated with Christ in heavenly places, and therefore I have access to what He has access to. And if heaven is the warehouse of earth's answers, there is nothing that I need that heaven does not have."

It Is Done

Before you even pray, the thing you are praying for already exists. You are not asking for something that has not yet been created. You are asking for something that was already prepared and waiting for you to announce its manifestation on the earth. Paul based this statement on that fact when he wrote, "For we are His workmanship, created in Christ Jesus for good works, which God prepared beforehand that we should walk in them" (Ephesians 2:10 NKJV).

When you pray for someone to receive healing, God does not say, "Okay, let Me think about how I am going to do this." No, the answer is already there. You simply access the place you are already in, which is heavenly places, and you say, "God, I know there is no sickness in heaven, so I am asking for the reality that is in heaven to be made manifest on earth. I am pulling healing from heaven to the earth." Then you will see the person you are praying for stand up out of a wheelchair and walk. Before you claimed that healing, God had already foreseen it. It did not surprise Him, and nobody had to jump through hoops to pray for it. That person's healing was a sovereign act of God, and you laid hold of it by praying from heavenly places, which is your place of prayer.

The Bible says Jesus was slain from the foundation of the world (see Revelation 13:8). That means Jesus' crucifixion was never plan B. When Adam and Eve sinned in the Garden of Eden, God did not have to scramble to correct the situation they had landed themselves in. He did not say, "Okay, well, I guess I will try a few things first, and then I will probably have to send Jesus." No, sending Jesus was His plan all along, so that He could receive the ultimate glory. We cannot comprehend the ins and outs of His will, but we can agree with it and work together with Him.

God moves according to His sovereign will, but He uses people on the earth through prayer and intercession to bring forth His plans. Jesus was always going to come to the earth, but God appointed people like Simeon and Anna to pray (Anna for as long as seventy years) so they could see the fulfillment of their prayers—the coming of the Messiah—the thing they had been interceding about for so long. Simeon and Anna were not praying for a new thing; they were praying for the thing that God had already spoken. God had already decided to send a savior, and when they prayed, heaven answered with Jesus. When we say, "Let Your will be done on earth as it is in heaven," we are calling for the answer to manifest on earth because it is already finished in heaven. We speak the prayers that unlock the door.

Praying Down Fire and Rain

Elijah knew how to pray like this better than almost anyone in the Bible. Remember when he took on the prophets of Baal? He challenged them on Mount Carmel, preparing an offering of two bulls and laying it on an altar (see 1 Kings 18). The challenge was to see whose god would set the offering on fire; they were not allowed to light the sacrificial fire themselves. The prophets of Baal were to call on their god and Elijah would call on his God, and whichever god answered by setting fire to the offering would be known as the true God in Israel.

Elijah was so confident in God that before he prayed, he had the wood on the altar doused with twelve jars of water. There was so much water that it saturated the altar and filled a trench surrounding it—and this was in the middle of a drought. Elijah was giving God an unusual offering in an inconvenient time. It was not convenient for him to give God water, but I believe he did that not only to prove just how powerful his God is—because He would soon ignite the altar that had been drenched—but also to give God even more glory. Everyone knows that when there is a battle between fire and water, water usually wins. Elijah was going to make sure that everyone recognized that God was powerful enough to flip that over completely.

God uses people on the earth through prayer and intercession to bring forth His plans.... He appointed people like Simeon and Anna to pray for seventy years so they could see the fulfillment of their prayers— the coming of the Messiah—the thing they had been interceding about for so long.

In addition, Elijah put that water on the altar because he knew he was about to pray a prayer of faith and place a demand on heaven by asking for rain to end the drought. To underline the fact he was going to ask God to do a supernatural thing and end the drought, he decided to give God an inconvenient sacrifice of water.

On Mount Carmel, Elijah gave God whatever he had, knowing that he was going to place a demand on heaven. He was so sure of heaven's response that he dared to wet the wood and taunt his rivals when they could not get their god to do anything. And he was more than vindicated, because the fire of God came and licked up everything, including the water itself, leaving only smoldering ashes.

This was only the first part. Immediately afterward, Elijah sought out King Ahab and boldly urged him to get ready to celebrate the upcoming breaking of the drought: "Go up, eat and drink; for there is the sound of abundance of rain" (1 Kings 18:41 NKJV). Had he heard the falling rain yet? Only in his spirit. So he applied himself to prayer to make it a physical reality. He knew what God was going to do, but he still had to go before the Lord and pray earnestly. The sound of rain could be heard only in the realm of the spirit, in heaven—until he prayed. Just because he heard the rain in the realms of heaven, he was not absolved of his responsibility to pray for it to be seen on the earth.

Prophecy does not excuse you from prayer; it informs your prayer. Elijah thought, *I know what I heard in the Spirit, but that does not allow me to become*

Prophecy does not excuse you from prayer; it informs your prayer.

lazy on the earth. I am going to partner with what heaven is already doing, so I can see the acceleration of it on the earth. And so he prayed, and at first he saw nothing in the sky (see 1 Kings 18:43–45). He kept praying, and he kept sending his servants to check for clouds. Six more times the servant looked, in vain. But the seventh time his servant went out and looked in the sky, he saw a cloud the size of a man's hand. That was enough for Elijah to get up from the place of prayer, because he knew if he saw the little thing—just the beginning—the full manifestation that God had promised was on its way.

Elijah heard something from heaven that compelled him to pray on the earth, in order to pull forth what was already done in heaven. Where was the rain contained? In heaven. You see, Elijah was asking for what already existed in heaven to fall on the earth. I love this story because it makes it so clear how this works. When you and I ask the Spirit of God to move for revival, for healing, for breakthrough, for deliverance, for life, for salvation, we are asking for what already exists in heaven.

Revised Paradigms

This was not the only time that Elijah pulled down to earth what he could see already in heaven. Reading about his exploits should change our expectations and our paradigms.

Remember the widow of Zarephath (see 1 Kings 17:8–16)? God brought Elijah to the house of the widow and her son during that severe drought, when they had just enough food left for one meal. They thought they were going to starve to death. Elijah told her to share with him the little she had, which took a lot of faith on her part. Then, because she acted in faith, God provided in abundance for her and her son. As long as the drought continued, there was always food in their house.

Paging forward in the Bible to the gospel of Matthew, we read about a time when Jesus came down from the mountain after preaching the Sermon on the Mount, and He encountered a man with leprosy (see Matthew 8). Lepers were considered unclean, and according to the Law, if someone touched a person with leprosy, that person would also become unclean. Leprosy was a very contagious disease. But Jesus reached out without hesitation and touched the leprous man (see Matthew 8:3).

The people watching this were witnessing the introduction of a new paradigm. In the Kingdom of God, instead of the unclean contaminating the clean, the clean destroys whatever makes a person unclean. This refers back to the Lord's Prayer: "Your kingdom come. Your will be done on the earth as it is in heaven." When we pray that, we are asking for the perfection of what already exists in heavenly places to overtake the reality of the dysfunction of earth.

Once I (Pastor Caleb) went on a trip for a few days, and when I returned home, my son ran to greet me. He had the stickiest fingers you have ever seen; I mean, it looked like he had been washing his hands in juice. Not only were they sticky, but lint and dirt had also gotten stuck all over his fingers.

The minute he saw me, my son came running, expecting me to pick him up. Now, on that particular day I was wearing a sweater that I did not want to get dirty. I could have said, "Hey, buddy, let's wash your hands first; then Daddy will pick you up." But no, I picked him up, and I hugged and kissed him. He did touch my sweater quite a bit, but oddly enough it did not get dirty, even though his hands looked so dirty.

Immediately the Holy Spirit said to my spirit, *Your dirtiness does not affect My cleanliness.* What He was saying was, "I am not affected by what is happening there. However, you will be affected by what happens up here."

I want to keep praying and asking for the perfection of *there* to be manifest *here*, because I know that what is happening in heaven will overtake whatever we see happening on earth, and that my prayers have an important part in that.

When you come into the presence of God, you may feel like my son with sticky hands that are all messed up. But your dirt cannot stop the Kingdom of God.

Because we are seated in heavenly places with Christ Jesus, we have the authority and the ability to effect change on the earth. We are not helpless. We are not stuck waiting for things to happen. We are not bystanders. We are not passive. No, we are playing an active role as the things of heaven become a reality on the earth because, again, God never intended for divine orchestration to happen without our human participation. He desires for us to be included. His plan involves His people, whose prayers bring His plans and purposes to pass.

This may be a new paradigm for us, but He wants it to become a lifestyle. The fact that it is already done in heaven does not mean we do not have to be persistent in prayer.

I believe God is calling us up higher and inviting us to think differently. He is inviting us to a place where we have a higher perspective. He certainly does not want us to ignore the reality of what is happening on earth, because He has a job for us—actively asking that the realities of heaven be imposed in the realities of earth. This is not some sort of mind trick. And it should not make us casual about the very real pain, dysfunction and harm that we experience on the earth.

When we are in the place of prayer, we choose not to be bound or limited by what we see here on the earth, because that is not where we hold our true citizenship. Our true citizenship is in heaven. Standing strong, we pray and pull what we can see in heaven down to the earth, and we ask that it will invade and transform the imperfection of earth.

PRAYER

Loving God, I know that You need no introduction to me, because You are my Creator and You know me inside out. However, I want to know You better—much better—than I do today. I would even say that I want to know You intimately. To achieve that closeness, I offer myself to You now and every day. Reveal to me the width and length and depth and height of Your love. Open the eyes of my heart to see that what I am praying for already exists in the spiritual realm. I am Yours forever. Because of Jesus, Amen.

9

Pray Until You See It

"Sing, O childless woman, you who have never given
birth! Break into loud and joyful song, O Jerusalem,
you who have never been in labor. For the desolate
woman now has more children than the woman who
lives with her husband," says the LORD.

Isaiah 54:1

If you are at Deeper Fellowship for five minutes, you will hear
the term *revival*. For us, revival is not an event; it is a culture
that welcomes the continual outpouring of the Holy Spirit.
In this environment, people are saved. Repentance is present.
Sick and diseased bodies are healed. The presence of God is
honored and revered. His Word is proclaimed. The gifts of
the Spirit are active. People are empowered. The awareness

of Christ is increased. The lost find hope in the risen Savior. In short, the church is alive.

This is revival, and it is happening within our church and around the world, but God has been saying to us that there is more, and we realize that this significant. Revival is not happening here only, but it is also spreading. God has given us the privilege of not only experiencing it for ourselves but of proclaiming revival prophetically to everyone everywhere. We do not take this for granted. It is a privilege to hear the prophetic word of the Lord and experience its fulfillment at the same time. We know this is not something that always happens.

This is what makes Isaiah 54 so interesting to us. In it, the prophet is proclaiming a future that he would not walk in himself. Earlier in the first part of the book of Isaiah, Isaiah himself was quite involved in both the proclamation and fulfilment of the word from the Lord. For example, we read in Isaiah 6:1, "It was in the year King Uzziah died that I saw the Lord. He was sitting on a lofty throne, and the train of his robe filled the Temple." For the first forty chapters of the book of Isaiah, the prophet has been actively engaged in the things he has been prophesying about. But later in the book, he begins to prophesy about things that would happen centuries after his death.

When we look at what he wrote in chapter 54, we see that Isaiah was prophesying restoration and revival, even though the circumstances that surrounded him at the time did not look anything like restoration and revival. The circumstances of those days were difficult indeed. God had been using the Assyrian army as a tool to chasten His people, who had gone astray, and eventually the people of Israel would become captives in Babylon. Yet Isaiah foresaw the end of all that, a time when the people would sing and rejoice. Thus the joyful proclamations of Isaiah 54.

Although we are prophesying revival here at Deeper Fellowship, it does not take a rocket scientist to see that much of the world is not experiencing anything like revival. Look around the world and what you will see does not necessarily look like an outpouring of God's Spirit. All the same, what Isaiah was talking about and what we are talking about are realities in the Spirit, even though we have yet to see them fully take root in the natural. This is one of the reasons we say we will not stop until we see it. We say that not because we have not seen it in our own midst—we have—but because our goal is for the whole world to experience it. We want the nations of the earth to experience the outpouring of the Spirit of God. For now God is inviting us to prophetically proclaim this reality.

That understanding is important. The Israelites were in a season of unfruitfulness. They were "barren." The Scripture says the barrenness was something that the Lord had brought on them, and it was something that the Lord subsequently healed. He did not allow them to be fruitful in rebellion because He did not want to raise up spiritual sons and daughters of rebellion. So when Isaiah says, "Sing O barren woman," he is literally saying, "God is about to allow you to birth spiritual sons and daughters in this next season. And when that time comes, I want you to begin to change your sound. I want you to be prepared to change your reality. I want you to shift the atmosphere where you are."

In rebellion, the Israelites were unfruitful. They were in idolatry. They had turned away from God. In fact, they were in captivity. Having been decimated by their enemies, they were bearing no spiritual fruit whatsoever.

Then Isaiah spoke, saying, "There is about to be a shift. Your sound is about to change from sorrow to joy. The womb that has been empty is about to become fruitful." In other words, "What you have been waiting for is about to burst forth. It is about to manifest. You have been hearing about a time coming in the future, but now is that time. Now is the time to get a song back in your heart, because revival is about to break forth at last!"

Prophets live in a place between declaration and manifestation.

It was a powerful prophetic declaration. However, Isaiah uttered it well before circumstances changed. Nothing looked like revival; that is for sure.

Like all prophets, Isaiah was proclaiming truths that had not yet come to pass. Prophets live in a place between declaration and manifestation. They dwell on the edge of spiritual reality, telling people to claim what God has promised right when nothing looks like the thing God has said He would do.

Between Declaration and Manifestation

What Isaiah prophesied had both an immediate result and an intermediate result, along with a future fulfillment. His words, recorded in Isaiah 54, spoke to his contemporaries within Israel, they spoke to a later generation and they also spoke of a future fulfillment. Paul appropriates Isaiah's words in his letter to the Galatians:

Tell me, you who desire to be under the law, do you not listen to the law? For it is written that Abraham had two sons, one

174

by a slave woman and one by a free woman. But the son of the slave was born according to the flesh, while the son of the free woman was born through promise. Now this may be interpreted allegorically: these women are two covenants. One is from Mount Sinai, bearing children for slavery; she is Hagar. Now Hagar is Mount Sinai in Arabia; she corresponds to the present Jerusalem, for she is in slavery with her children. But the Jerusalem above is free, and she is our mother. For it is written, *"Rejoice, O barren one who does not bear; break forth and cry aloud, you who are not in labor! For the children of the desolate one will be more than those of the one who has a husband."*

Now you, brothers, like Isaac, are children of promise. But just as at that time he who was born according to the flesh persecuted him who was born according to the Spirit, so also it is now. But what does the Scripture say? "Cast out the slave woman and her son, for the son of the slave woman shall not inherit with the son of the free woman." So, brothers, we are not children of the slave but of the free woman.

Galatians 4:21–32 ESV, emphasis added

We see here the intermediate fulfillment of Isaiah's prophecy, which was the inclusion, by faith in Christ, of the Gentiles as the children of Abraham and heirs to God's promise. Earlier, the word had been fulfilled when the Israelites came out of their captivity in Babylonia and became fruitful again, because God restored them. Now we are looking for the fulfillment that is yet to come, the establishment of the Kingdom of God on earth.

This is the tension of prophecy. When God speaks something over your life, the declaration of His word must somehow connect to its manifestation. Something must bridge the two. We see this "something" in the life of the prophet Elijah.

Elijah declared the word of the Lord to King Ahab: "Now Elijah, who was from Tishbe in Gilead, told King Ahab, 'As surely as the LORD, the God of Israel, lives—the God I serve—there will be no dew or rain during the next few years until I give the word!'" (1 Kings 17:1). Here you have a prophet who is declaring the word of the Lord, saying, "This is what is going to happen." Looking at this solely in the context of this account, all you see in this verse is a declaration of a prophetic word: It was not going to rain again until the prophet Elijah said so. But something had to happen between the declaration of that word and its manifestation.

James 5:17 says, "Elijah was as human as we are, and yet when he prayed earnestly that no rain would fall, none fell for three and a half years!" Elijah prayed earnestly that no rain would fall, and his prayers were answered. Elijah declared, and then he prayed earnestly.

Prayer is the "something" in the middle between declaration and manifestation. At Deeper Fellowship, we have taken this to heart. We are an apostolic and a prophetic house, which means that God uses our voices to speak things into the atmosphere by declaration. We have learned to declare the word of the Lord, and we have learned how to contend in prayer for its fulfillment. A while back, the Lord had the members of Deeper Fellowship study prayer for 21 weeks, and that changed us into a people who could and would bridge that gap between declaration and manifestation. We continue to learn how to hear God and declare His promises, and then to receive what has been declared.

You can apply this to your own life. God has not only been speaking to you; He is giving you the key for how to receive the things He has been declaring to you. He is giving you the key for possessing the promises of God, and that key is prayer.

Raise Your Expectations

Let's take a closer look at Elijah's declaration and manifestation in 1 Kings 18:

> Then Elijah said to Ahab, "Go get something to eat and drink, for I hear a mighty rainstorm coming!" So Ahab went to eat and drink. But Elijah climbed to the top of Mount Carmel and bowed low to the ground and prayed with his face between his knees.
>
> Then he said to his servant, "Go and look out toward the sea."
>
> The servant went and looked, then returned to Elijah and said, "I didn't see anything."
>
> Seven times Elijah told him to go and look. Finally the seventh time, his servant told him, "I saw a little cloud about the size of a man's hand rising from the sea."
>
> Then Elijah shouted, "Hurry to Ahab and tell him, 'Climb into your chariot and go back home. If you don't hurry, the rain will stop you!'"
>
> And soon the sky was black with clouds. A heavy wind brought a terrific rainstorm, and Ahab left quickly for Jezreel. Then the LORD gave special strength to Elijah. He tucked his cloak into his belt and ran ahead of Ahab's chariot all the way to the entrance of Jezreel.
>
> Verses 41–46

Here we see declaration is followed by expectation. Without expectation, you can actually kill the progression to manifestation. Expectation is the fuel that moves declaration toward manifestation across the bridge of prayer.

Believe me when I say that God wants you to be delivered from low expectations. Jesus was dealing with the low expectations of His disciples when He cursed the fig tree (see Mark 11:20–25). He was teaching them how to activate a combination of declaration and prayer by means of their expectant faith.

We see another example of the importance of expectation in Jesus' story about the farmer planting seed:

> Jesus also said, "The Kingdom of God is like a farmer who scatters seed on the ground. Night and day, while he's asleep or awake, the seed sprouts and grows, but he does not understand how it happens. The earth produces the crops on its own. First a leaf blade pushes through, then the heads of wheat are formed, and finally the grain ripens. And as soon as the grain is ready, the farmer comes and harvests it with a sickle, for the harvest time has come."
>
> Mark 4:26–29

The farmer scattered seed and he expected a harvest, even though he did not know how it would happen. Although he did not know how the seed would grow, he rested in the fact that seed sown produces a harvest; he simply expected it to happen. He knew that the harvest time would come.

In the same way, whenever a seed of the Word is planted, we can expect a harvest.

We cannot continue to plant the seeds of the Word forever, and we cannot do it without expecting at some point that a harvest will come. Lack of expectation has got to be one of the reasons some believers get so tired and weary in the faith. The preachers are constantly telling them, "God is getting ready. . . . God is getting ready. . . . God is getting ready." Okay, but at some point there must be a harvest time. At some point there has to be a manifestation. People get worn out from constant reminders about what God is getting ready to do without ever actually seeing any harvest.

Nobody can maintain that level of fight and faith. There has to be fulfillment, manifestation—some kind of a harvest. Let's allow our expectation level to rise. Let's believe we are entering a time of manifestation, a time of answers. Let's believe, expectantly and by the Spirit of God, that God is getting ready to perform the things He has spoken about.

None of us can make supernatural things happen on our own, any more than the farmer can force the seeds to produce a harvest. The process of the fulfillment of God's promises must rest entirely in God's capable hands. The manifestation will not usually come in our timing, but we have to do our part and trust God to do the rest.

We need to avoid the all-too-common response of waiting until conditions have improved (or are perfect) to put our full faith in God's promises: "Okay, I know God spoke to me, but until I get a degree, until I get things in place financially, until I get married . . ." Doing so essentially makes the word of the Lord null and void. It is as though, when God speaks something to us, we stop and assess the conditions before we plant the word, and then we often hesitate to plant it at all.

The Bible addresses this: "Farmers who wait for perfect weather never plant. If they watch every cloud, they never harvest" (Ecclesiastes 11:4). If you are trying to assess when and how you think God can do what He promised, you will never actually plant, and if you do not plant, you will not harvest. Do not choke out your expectation!

Ecclesiastes 11 goes on to say,

> Just as you cannot understand the path of the wind or the mystery of a tiny baby growing in its mother's womb, so you cannot understand the activity of God, who does all things. Plant your seed in the morning and keep busy all afternoon, for you don't know if profit will come from one activity or another—or maybe both.
>
> Verses 5–6

Do this because, as Proverbs 20:4 says, "Those too lazy to plow in the right season will have no food at the harvest." If you are too lazy to plow or pray or wait with faithful expectation, you are going to be hungry both naturally and spiritually.

The Progression toward Manifestation

We saw a progression in the account about Elijah and the rain, from prophecy to prayer to the clear manifestation of the results (see 1 Kings 18:41–46).

First Elijah prophesied what he heard—the sound of the abundance of rain. In general, prophets hear the word of the Lord; the prophets who see more than they hear are called seers. When Elijah heard, he prophesied what he heard. But he knew that in order to see the manifestation of his declaration, he had to do something else. So with complete assurance that what he had just declared would indeed come to pass shortly, he told the king to get ready. And Elijah applied himself to prayer. Only by those means would God's word come to pass.

A manifestation is a demonstration of power. No wonder you need to work up to it with persistent and even fervent prayer. The progression toward a manifestation is straightforward, but you cannot expect it to culminate in a victory unless you pray and pray and pray some more. You need to keep your focus. Just as Elijah's servant kept checking for rain clouds at Elijah's behest, so we must pray with expectation until we see real evidence of an answer. This is not complicated, but you cannot do it in your own strength. The whole time you are praying, you must keep the original word from the Lord in mind. What was His promise, His declaration? Pray it in.

Ask the Holy Spirit to direct your prayers and to give you the determined strength that you will need. Sometimes you will not need to pray very long, but sometimes you will need to keep praying for years. Sometimes you will be able to pray a thing through on your own, but other times you will want to shoulder the task alongside your brothers and sisters.

At times, God will speak to you about your future or your children's future. The manifestation or fulfillment of His words will not just happen. We participate through our prayers. I am thinking of a couple at our church who always spoke prophetic words over both of their children since they were small. After having grown up saturated in the things of God, their son went away to college, where he recognized that one of his classmates had a demon. He called his dad to tell him about it, and his dad was like, "Okay, I'm on it. I am on my way down." (This couple loves to cast out demons.)

But the son said, "Dad, don't worry about it. I already took care of it." He and his roommate had already cast the demon out.

That would not have happened if his parents had not prayed so faithfully and fervently. Somebody had to pray. Between declaration and manifestation, there has to be prayer. This may seem elementary, but if you do not get this, you will not see the manifestation of the word God has spoken. The next time you hear the word of the Lord and start to get excited, be sure not just to assume it will happen without your participation. Yes, it may be an awesome word, but turn your initial expectation into long-term, faith-filled prayer. Do something about it. Contend for it. You will surely be rewarded.

Pray Until . . .

Elijah said, "God said it is going to rain," and he told his servant to look at the sky to see what was happening. That is expectation. But did his expectation die when the servant did not see rain the first time he looked?

When people pray for healing, they must not allow pain or other evidences of their illness to stop them from believing. They must maintain their expectation and keep praying. People can have expectation in the face of pain. In fact, many times the pain will not disappear after the first prayer—or the second or the third. Only if they pray until the pain disappears can they stop praying. "God, You said that by Your stripes we are healed. We are staying here, believing for healing, even if we do not see it right away. We keep praying." One, two, three, four, five, six times, you cannot predict how much prayer it will take. Elijah's servant returned to his viewpoint to check for rain clouds seven times before he saw "a little cloud about the size of a man's hand," but that was enough.

Elijah had not been deterred, because he knew what God had said. He was determined to pray with his face to the ground until the manifestation of what he had heard could be seen with human eyes. And when he saw the first evidence of an answer, then (and only then) he moved. When you see any sign of an answer, even if the complete fulfillment is still far off, that is the time to get moving, because your manifestation is on its way.

Prayer is the bridge between declaration and manifestation. Both expectation and preparation travel on that bridge. Both of them put legs under the manifestation.

Now, here is something interesting: Elijah sent his servant as a messenger to the king to tell him that he had better get going because if he did not, the rain would stop him. In other words, the very thing he needed (rain) had the potential to stop him. In the same way, the full manifestation of the thing you have been praying and waiting for can actually stop your forward movement if you do not prepare.

Let's think about how this can apply to our situations. We must prepare for revival by learning how to pray and by sharpening our teaching and discipling skills. We must prepare for promotion in our jobs by acquiring new skills. We must prepare for increase by being faithful stewards of what we already have. We do both: prepare and pray.

As we have been saying, prayer is the bridge between declaration and manifestation. Both expectation and preparation travel on that bridge. Both of them put legs under the manifestation.

We should expect to see answers to prayer. Between declaration and manifestation, we have a responsibility to believe. And we have a responsibility to pray. Prayer is the bridge. So awaken your expectation, and prepare for manifestation.

Put Your Confidence in God

Your prayer life is being unlocked in this season. I believe God is getting ready to birth something through your prayers and the collective prayers of the Body of Christ that will radically change lives, communities, regions and nations. God is getting ready to blow you away as it relates to your future, and you are not going to miss what He has for you. He is going to allow you to experience the joy of answered prayer.

The apostle John wrote,

> I have written this to you who believe in the name of the Son of God, so that you may know you have eternal life. And we are confident that he hears us whenever we ask for anything that pleases him. And since we know he hears us when we make our requests, we also know that he will give us what we ask for.
>
> 1 John 5:13–15

Of all the things John could have said, he decided to end this letter by encouraging people to pray. He did that because he wanted his readers to become fully awake and fully alive to the reality that the God of heaven was interacting with them. The same God who said "I will never leave you nor forsake you" is the One who hears and answers our prayers.

Know that when you pray to Him, He hears you. Nothing is a better proof of God's love for you. Whenever you go through times of adversity and pressure, remember that everyone who has eternal life has access to God. Having access guarantees answers to your prayers because the God who gave you eternal life is also the God who hears your prayers. Knowing that God hears you gives you confidence. You will never stop praying because God's loving response is not based on your personal goodness; it is based on His goodness. And God's desire to be good to you in the future is not based upon how good you are right now; it is based upon what Jesus did two thousand years ago.

God worked out a way to provide you with the ultimate security before you even realized it was needed. Therefore, since your ultimate security is certain, you can be sure that He is looking out for your future on earth.

God decided to give you heaven. But He also decided to give you what you need on the earth. So begin to ask Him for what you need, and begin to join your prayers with the prayers of others for revival.

The world is dying for lack of prayers. Let's do our part to show how it is done.

PRAYER

Glorious God, my heart's desire is to follow You closely all the days of my life, praying and trusting and participating in Your Kingdom life here on earth. Whether or not my every prayer is answered visibly during my time on earth, may my declaration of Your Word bring about the full manifestation of Your will. Every prayer rings with the same theme: May You bring heaven to earth and invite as many people as possible to live with You forever. In Jesus' powerful name, Amen.

Notes

Chapter 1 Don't Just Want It—Pray for It

1. Blue Letter Bible, s.v. "*synantilambanomai*," accessed July 13, 2019, https://www.blueletterbible.org/lang/Lexicon/Lexicon.cfm?strongs=G4878&t=KJV.

Chapter 2 Intimacy—The Key to Your Authority

1. Blue Letter Bible, s.v. "*menō*," accessed January 4, 2019, https://www.blueletterbible.org/lang/lexicon/lexicon.cfm?t=kjv&strongs=g3306.

2. "Expecting"; lyrics by William McDowell, with David Binion and Joshua Dufrene.

3. Fornication is typically an outgrowth of not being satisfied with Jesus. The hunger of the flesh plays its part, but for believers who are fornicating, it is typically not only because they have not put their flesh in check but also because they are not satisfied with Jesus. So they need somebody else to give them affection and affirmation.

Chapter 3 Prayer—The Language of Faith

1. Kevin DeYoung, "Prayerlessness Is Unbelief," The Gospel Coalition, November 6, 2009, https://www.thegospelcoalition.org/blogs/kevin-deyoung/prayerlessness-is-unbelief/.

2. John Calvin as quoted in Jon Bloom, "What to Do When We're Prayerless," Desiring God, January 23, 2015, https://www.desiringgod.org/articles/what-to-do-when-were-prayerless.

3. Jon Bloom, "What to Do When We're Prayerless," Desiring God, January 23, 2015, https://www.desiringgod.org/articles/what-to-do-when -were-prayerless.

Chapter 4 Ten Hindrances to Answered Prayer

1. Kendra Cherry, "Locus of Control and Your Life," Verywell Mind, June 4, 2019, https://www.verywellmind.com/what-is-locus-of-control -2795434.

2. *The Preacher's Outline & Sermon Bible: Hebrews, James* (Chattanooga, Tenn.: Leadership Ministries Worldwide, 1996), 303.

Chapter 5 Ten Benefits of Prayer

1. Sinclair Ferguson, "What Is the Prayer of Faith?" Ligonier Ministries, April 15, 2020, https://www.ligonier.org/blog/prayer-faith/.

Chapter 6 The Divine Council

1. Righteousness is imputed to us by faith in Christ, and that is the book of Romans in a nutshell. We have been made right with God by placing our faith in Jesus Christ. People who lived before Christ came were considered righteous based on their level of right living. That is why the Bible says that God took Abraham's faith and accounted it to him as righteousness (see Genesis 15:6). Abraham had faith to believe that God could raise the dead. This was critically important because for Abraham to believe God would raise the dead meant he was actually peering into the future and seeing the day in which God would overcome death. He believed that a way would be made to overcome death, the great enemy of humankind, and God counted this faith as righteousness.

William McDowell is a gifted teacher and world-renowned, Grammy-nominated, Dove and Stellar Award-winning worship leader who has ministered in more than fifty nations. He is the lead pastor of Deeper Fellowship Church, a growing congregation in Orlando, Florida. He is also the author of *It's Happening* and is an in-demand speaker throughout the world. His ability to cross generational, denominational, cultural and genre differences is a reflection of his heart for people and his foundational ministry training. He and his wife have five children.

Jason McMullen is the executive pastor of Deeper Fellowship Church. A prophetic voice and seasoned strategist, Jason is also the president of McMullen Ventures. He considers his greatest professional achievement to be the launch of the Modern English Bible, which is an updated literal translation of the King James Bible. He and his wife reside in Orlando, Florida, with their ten children.

Caleb Grant is an associate pastor of Deeper Fellowship Church. With an insatiable hunger for God, Caleb is both a committed prophet and preacher. In addition to his responsibilities at Deeper Fellowship Church, Caleb travels, teaching and ministering to people around the world. He and his wife reside in Orlando, Florida, with their two children.